I ALMOST MADE IT

a memoir

I ALMOST MADE IT

a memoir

Peter Graves

GREEN WRITERS PRESS *Brattleboro, Vermont*

Copyright © 2025 Peter Graves

All rights reserved. No part of this book may be reproduced in any form or by any means, electronic or mechanical, including photocopying, recording, or by any information storage and retrieval system, without permission in writing from the publisher.

Printed in the United States

10 9 8 7 6 5 4 3 2 1

Green Writers Press is a Vermont-based publisher whose mission is to spread a message of hope and renewal through the words and images we publish. Throughout we will adhere to our commitment to preserving and protecting the natural resources of the earth. To that end, a percentage of our proceeds will be donated to environmental activist groups. Green Writers Press gratefully acknowledges support from individual donors, friends, and readers to help support the environment and our publishing initiative.

GReen
wriTers
press

Giving Voice to Writers & Artists Who Will Make the World a Better Place
Green Writers Press | Brattleboro, Vermont • www.greenwriterspress.com

ISBN: 979-8-9914134-9-7

BOOK & COVER DESIGN BY
ALLISON PINEAULT

All photos courtesy of the author unless otherwise credited.

PRINTED ON PAPER WITH PULP THAT COMES FROM FSC-CERTIFIED FORESTS, MANAGED FORESTS THAT GUARANTEE RESPONSIBLE ENVIRONMENTAL, SOCIAL, AND ECONOMIC PRACTICES. ALL WOOD PRODUCT COMPONENTS USED IN BLACK & WHITE, STANDARD COLOR, OR SELECT COLOR PAPERBACK BOOKS, UTILIZING EITHER CREAM OR WHITE BOOKBLOCK PAPER ARE SUSTAINABLE FORESTRY INITIATIVE® (SFI®) CERTIFIED SOURCING.

For my wonderful adult children, Willy and Katie, and for Grandson James with love. My loving parents, Van and Ella Graves, and Aunt Oddie. Thank you, Bucky, for giving me my first pair of cross-country skis, and instruction on the meaning of them. Thank you for believing in me even when I did not. And to all who encouraged me in this journey and all those that opened doors for me during my career.

CONTENTS

Introduction	*1*
Let's Start at the Beginning	11
The Early Days	25
Fort Lewis	37
Durango Broadcasting Blastoff	49
Another Move, This Time to Telemark	59
Notur Daze and the Phone Call	71
ABC and My First Olympic Games	79
ESPN: The Early Days	93
Photo Section	102
1992 Olympics at TNT	119
Salt Lake City	127
Harvard Skiing	137
OLN	145
Athens	153

On to WCSN, Universal, and NBC Sports	161
Off to Holmenkollen: A Dream Come True	177
Korea: The 13th Games	183
That's All Folks	193
Afterword	203
Acknowledgments	*205*
About the Author	*209*

*For of all the sad words of tongue or pen,
the saddest are these: It might have been.*

—John Greenleaf Whittier

I ALMOST MADE IT

a memoir

INTRODUCTION

1

Why is someone like me writing a book? It makes little sense to me. What forever for? My life wasn't so different from anyone else's. It was no better, no worse, and yet it's a story of someone fighting back against big odds to make something of my life. From a small Vermont town, I still don't feel especially gifted, talented, or blessed with some unique set of skills, and yet inside me there are stories. And some may even prove instructive, as in, everyone has a good story to tell.

Yet one thing's certain: I dared to dream big, and I never gave up on those dreams. Sometimes my aspirations failed to be realized, and I'm okay with that. Don't many Little League players dream to be in the Majors?

This book is not intended to be curative, nor glib. Neither is it intended to be a triumphal tale of overcoming some adversity, as I had little, except what I conjured up myself. We all take a few steps forward and a few backward. I've done both. At times I've been elated, at times broken, but I've not been defeated. The truth is, no matter how far your career takes you, we all end up in the same place. We are, in fact, small potatoes in the scheme of things. All of us.

I love people and always have. I've seen honor and nobility aplenty from regular folk without fancy college degrees. If you grew up in rural America, you know what I mean. I love small towns around the world and the charm that always exists there. From the Alps to Japan, and from Cairns, Australia, to Capetown, I've been lucky to visit them all, and have made warm friendships that have been long lasting as a result. What's more, since I was always on a broadcasting assignment, I not only had the luxury of having all my travel paid for, but I was paid to do the job. How nice.

Lest one think it's been an altogether smooth ride, I've dealt with my share of heartache and pain. I am a cancer survivor, and have been married three times, something I'm not especially proud of; and since the age of sixty, I've been in chronic pain of neuropathy in my feet, which makes getting around challenging. It hasn't been something I've talked a great deal about for fear of losing announcing jobs or boring my friends with my aches and pains. Yet it's become the greatest physical struggle I've ever known. Further, there is no cure for small fiber neuropathy and little in the way of pain control. So, like so many things in life, it's the luck of the draw and one simply sucks it up and moves forward. It sounds a little like broadcasting and announcing to me.

Life, and especially broadcasting, is not a linear line of constant achievement. For you—like everyone else that's honest and reflective—would note that you win some, you lose some, and some get rained out. Further, regardless of seeing yourself as bulletproof, understand that one day it will end.

My goals were extraordinarily high. If I couldn't fill the chair of broadcasting heroes like Jim McKay or Bob Costas, why even try? I was to learn on my journey that those were near impossible goals to attain. But at least I shot for the stars, as they say. Somehow I processed that if I wasn't in that circle, I would be a failure. What hubris on my part. Still, that offers a look into my own motivations for my life's path.

I wished I had read more Robert Frost when I was younger, for he wrote about the seriousness of how we hold things, our desires. For so long, my wants were so powerful I didn't enjoy everything as I might have. I didn't laugh enough. I didn't always see that, in fact, it really is all a game. As Frost noted, "Work becomes play with mortal stakes."

Being somewhat insecure as a performer, I often envisioned that failure was just beyond the next corner. Please understand this and learn from me: it all takes some measure of bravery. It's up to you to create your own truth. There will be good times and bad. Try not to vomit from nerves at ski races like I often did as a kid.

I tried all along to achieve something, god knows what. I didn't lie or hoodwink anyone, but I had an abundance of energy, drive, and curiosity about the world. With little broadcasting experience, I worked for ABC Sports at the Olympic Games when I was twenty-five. I Spent fifteen years freelancing for ESPN, and decades as a freelance broadcaster. I wanted the work so much I could have tasted it, and through it all, despite being close to my goal, I have reflected much to come to the conclusion that . . . "I Almost Made It."

LET'S START AT THE BEGINNING

2

A fanatic is one who can't change his mind and won't change the subject.

—Winston Churchill

I was born and raised in the Vermont town of Bennington, the only child of Van and Ella Graves, who became parents at an older age. Dad was a lawyer and a judge, and I grew up in a neighborhood populated by boys of my age, all baby boomers. We were constantly in motion and I recall it as an ideal childhood. I was born into a family of some privilege, although they wore that mantle in the most unassuming way. Never a new car, or fancy foods. My Dad's good taste and upbringing was modified by my mother's Irish heritage of down-to-earthiness. Think PBR. Even today I still like that mixture.

For as long as I can remember, this freckle-faced, red-haired boy that I once recall as myself was an eager, engaging, and curious kid. I wanted to try everything. I was captivated by sport of all kinds, but especially skiing, which was deeply embedded in my Vermont roots.

First I suppose it was in the backyard and later on a neighbor's hill, then the rope tow at Leake's farm, and finally up the mountain from Bennington to Prospect Mountain in Woodford, Vermont. Both of my parents skied for fun and had been doing it since the late 1920s. They enjoyed the peace of sliding around on skis in nearby Woodford, a snow-drenched place where their friend Alec Drysdale had carved some trails out of the lush forest and ran a Model T Ford engine for a crude rope tow. They never talked of racing, but simply the joy of being out in winter. For my parents relished the sight of new-fallen snow and the winter winds.

I still love Prospect. It's an intimate, cozy place, the kind where there's always a wood fire and wool socks hanging to dry, a particularly pungent smell that makes me feel like I'm home. All of us kids— and here I mean most everyone—had the chance if they wanted to ski at Prospect Mountain. A windy seven-mile drive up the twisting highway and a large gain in elevation would bring you to another world. It was a snow-drenched paradise. If anyone had natural snow, Prospect did, and we were blessed to have an inexpensive place to ski and hang out. The smell of winter woodsmoke, of Halsey's cigar at the ticket booth, the sound of Tyrolean music, and Dom's hot meatball sandwiches at the snack bar afforded us kids a joyous experience, a love of winter, and now what can only be described as a transformative experience. I will never, as long as I live, forget those happy, carefree, joyous days. What was even better was to have my friends with me on this journey. It crossed cultural and economic lines. Vermont kids could ski cheap and carefree. As I have grown older it affects me greatly to see that skiing from a cost perspective is simply out of the realm for many now. It really pains me to see that. It's a problem that affects American ski racing too.

My parents were the most wonderful, loving parents, who nurtured in their only child a kind of love and acceptance that proved to be most unusual, and with a strong bond that lasted for me until they passed away. Not only did I experience the purest form of love and acceptance from them, but they supported my dreams financially too. Unlike many of my high school friends, I was the beneficiary of a large net to catch me if I fell. It allowed me the distinct privilege of following my dreams. Not every kid could do that, and I felt truly blessed by the advantages afforded me. There were spring vacation trips to New York and the theater; there were monthly summer vacations at Weekapaug, Rhode Island, and trips to Florida. Still, at the time, it just seemed all normal.

My mother, Ella, was an early champion of women's sports, playing basketball in high school, later to become the coach at Ben-High in Bennington, and later to be a very fine golfer who played into her nineties. She was loving and protecting, a teacher of manners and adult conversation, and she was my greatest champion. My father was a kind and gentle man who lacked the aggressiveness of my Mom, but did the worrying for both of them. He did much pro bono work for locals in town in need of legal advice, and was the most honest and ethical man I ever met. He didn't go to too many of my races—not because he wasn't interested, but instead because he was always worried about seeing me fail and get hurt. Together, they provided me with a safe, happy, and nurturing upbringing, and I never heard either of them yell. Really.

From as far back as I can remember, I had the feeling that I wanted to excel in something, and for me it manifested itself in sport. Not that it came easy, of course, and not that it came before a great deal of introspection.

I was the product of a public school education. However, I spent two unhappy years at a private school in Williamstown, MA, away from my friends and for the first time truly challenged academically. I couldn't wait to leave. So, after fifth and sixth grade, my parents decided that I should return to Ben-High, where I started seventh grade with my peer group from before.

When I returned, I'm not sure what I had expected, but I started getting teased a lot. I think this proved very painful, but also formative. I wanted to matter and I wanted the attention. Teased in the locker room as adolescent boys tend to do, teased at football practice. Eggs smashed in my face, I got beaten up a few times by the local young toughs from town. I still can't understand why. For those years, I pondered, why don't people like me? Looking around, it seemed like the popular boys were jocks, so I became one. They also got girlfriends. It looked as simple as that.

But when I was in the Little League baseball tryouts, I got promptly cut from the squad due— in the coaches' minds—to lack of ability. That hurt my aching adolescent self-esteem. I tried out for junior high football, and although I made the team, I didn't play much and recall much of that experience as being largely negative. Still, it didn't kill my drive. So, truth be told, I was processing a lot of data that I wasn't a very good athlete. Which could be translatable into being not very good at anything that mattered.

But late at night through my transistor radio, I was captivated by the sound of radio stations coursing through my tiny ear piece. It gave me a window to the world. I would listen to the big-time DJs at major markets like WLS Chicago, CKLW in Windsor, Ontario/Detroit, or WKBW in Buffalo. The vibrancy of top-forty radio was so big, and I loved everything, from the way the jocks riffed with words to their jingles. Think Cousin Brucie with his rapid-fire delivery. It almost made the hair on my arms stand. If it wasn't top-forty, I'd listen to far-away baseball contests like the Red Sox games from Fenway with Ken Coleman and Ned Martin, trying to emulate softly what magic I was hearing.

Then in 1966, Bucky Broomhall, of the famous Broomhall skiing clan of Rumford, Maine, came to Bennington. His arrival in my hometown most certainly changed the course of my life, I'm sure of that. I, of course, didn't realize how lucky I was.

As for many kids of the day, we were encouraged

to ski in all events. I had a head start with Alpine skiing, which my parents introduced me to at about age three or four. There was jumping, which was hard to get used to, as I never considered myself the daring type. Then, on the first day of dryland training that fall, Bucky told us about a new kind of skiing: cross-country.

I won't say cross-country skiing was love at first site, but there was something there that suited me. I liked the fitness required to excel, and the repetitive movement seemed to be a soothing balm for my ofttimes fiery Irish temperament. I truly had no idea what it really was, but I learned fast and worked hard, and by my junior year I had started to achieve some basic mastery of the sport. After having been a half-rate talent in football, soccer, and baseball, I yearned to find something that I could find some measure of mastery and athletic success in. And to be sure, I longed to find something that would impress the girls.

At first, I began to articulate an image of running on skis, rather than gliding. Once I began to learn about gliding on skis, I became much more efficient. Yet it took hard work and concentration to master it. I had plenty of practice falling on the downhills, but a face full of snow is oftentimes a delightful feeling. Whizzing down the hills with the trees just over my shoulders made me feel like I was mastering the sport, and that I had discovered something truly exhilarating. In that era snow was abundant and it felt like skiing in a winter wonderland.

Above all, then, XC skiing required a high level of fitness, and I was not afraid of training hard to achieve success. I seemed to be able to push myself and endure the pain, if that's what it took to be good. I've always thought those that train for XC skiing come in two distinct blends: those that train because they love training, and those that train hard because that is the price of being good in the sport.

Slowly, my peers began to take notice of my skiing results. The more they did, the harder I worked. Still, it was tendered by a genuine love of being outside in winter with my friends. For me, it wasn't just about being a good athlete, but I also just wanted to fit in, like most do at that age. I would entertain my skiing teammates in the van, with my mock radio shows. They liked it (thankfully), and it sure made the hours fly by. I was captivated, and it seemed like something that I'd like to try. I loved broadcasting, but I also loved skiing.

One day for my birthday, my parents gave me a small amplifier and microphone. It wasn't long before I started, from my bedroom window, broad-

I Almost Made It

casting make-believe sports to the surrounding neighborhood. I don't recall anyone telling me to shut it off. I was hooked. I paid special attention to phrasing, punching out sentences and word choices as I tried to emulate my heroes of the airwaves. Television was growing but radio was the king. It was fast talking, cool, and drew much attention for those of us coming of age, even if my parents were mildly perplexed.

Our team began to make progress. The trails at Prospect had to be largely developed, nestled amongst the fragrant pine forest and small lakes that abound in Woodford, Vermont. There had to be the right mix of skiable terrain, and then a good course had to have a blend of uphill, downhill, and flat and rolling—one third of each. Once that work was done, we had to ski in the tracks necessary for classic skiing. It took time, but it resonated deeply within my heart and soul. With great coaching and real teamwork, we improved with every passing race. It became something that was life affirming. Most import of all was our willingness to learn. This was years before skating on skis became a separate discipline, so we forged ahead to learn the basics of classic cross-country technique. Slowly the sport began to grow at Mt. Anthony, and we became the surprise of the circuit. The team there is still a top performer in Vermont state, and a number of Olympians have come out of the program.

I was especially blessed to have a close friend with me. My journey through high school and beyond was made all the better as I was able to share it with my lifelong friend, Robin Outwater. Together, we shared many sports experiences, the oftentimes challenging slings and arrows of growing up, and now the rigors of aging. He has been a true blessing in my life. But athletically he pushed me, as I pushed him, and it made us both better on skis. Yet, as an overall athlete Robin was without peer; he was one of the most naturally talented athletes I ever came across; he could do anything.

I look at the era, unbeknownst to me then, as the happiest of my life. Isn't that always the way?

THE EARLY DAYS

3

By the end of my junior year, Bucky Broomhall had left his Nordic-ski-coaching position at the high school, and in came a Norwegian named Birger Vigsnes. Birger was to be both the soccer and skiing coach. He had skied at St. Lawrence University and, like Bucky, came with impressive credentials. I feel lucky to have had their influences in my life. Both Bucky and Birger were fine coaches, and I learned the basics of technique, tactics, and fitness. I always felt short on true athletic talent, but I learned to work hard and I was super fit and motivated, which in that era was an immense advantage. I also learned about the value of sportsmanship.

Being that the then-epicenter of the US Nordic universe was a scant forty miles away from Bennington in Putney, and that they skied in our high school league, it was then only logical that I would run into Johnny Caldwell. JC (as he was called) coached at the Putney School, was a national team and Olympic coach, and was the noted author of the Cross-Country Ski Book, a tome that would make a huge impression on me. JC got a big kick out of my eagerness, as did other hallowed members of the US National Team in those halcyon days. I probably bugged the shit out of him, but he didn't let on. I called him—begged to come to training camps in Putney and beyond. In the summer of 1969, he graciously allowed me to tag along for a USST hike on Vermont's Long Trail.

Here I was in the midst of my heroes: Mike Gallagher, Bob Gray, Mike Elliott, Ned Gillette, and so many others. The day I joined the team we speed-hiked from Manchester to near Bennington. It was great fun. This was the flower of my youth.

The following summer Johnny relented to let me join the team's annual summer soiree, riding racing bikes around New England. This proved an eye opener for me, as I had never seen a racing bike, and showed up with sneakers, tennis shorts, and my three-speed Schwinn. Don't let them tell you I

I ALMOST MADE IT

had streamers on the bar ends or baseball cards in the spokes—that became the stuff of a legendary spoof the team did on me once that got better and better with every telling.

I learned a lot that day. I should have been embarrassed, but I wasn't, and JC kept picking me up and placing me back with the field. I was thrilled and captivated, and my parents were happy too. Caldwell would play a major role as a mentor to me in my skiing and in my life as a dear friend.

Trips to his sauna became, too, the stuff of legend. Frankly, I was a sponge just eating it all up, with a grin from ear to ear. The gossip, the stories, and just hangin' with my heroes told me I had arrived—or more precisely, that I was accepted. Oftentimes the big guns of the sport were there, taking in the heat and engaging in captivating tales of life on the race circuit. I was all ears.

The wood heat of the sauna, followed by a cold-water plunge in Johnny's crystal-clear pond, was one of the most sublime experiences of my life that lasted but a minute. It was clean, pure, and simple. Plus, I thought, if you made it—got invited to this special sauna in Putney, Vermont, that now sits idle—you were truly among the anointed. It felt great to be included, sitting next to my idols of sport. People like Bob Gray, Mike Eliott, Mike

Gallagher, Charlie Kellogg and Martha Rockwell were among them.

The stories painted a rich life, including the rigors of off-season training, dining on European foods, staying in nice hotels, attempts for many fumbling with fractured German language skills (those who were fluent had a leg up on everyone else), long drives, and scary tram rides at the Dachstein Glacier. Much of the chatter also centered on the political side of the sport, especially regarding USSA, the national governing body of the sport (now known as the US Ski and Snowboard Association, headquartered in Park City, Utah). It was so powerful to me to be included amongst this group, and it caused my dreams to soar. I continued to focus on my own personal improvements in the sport. I wanted more.

My senior year, I focused laser-like on the next step up the progression ladder and set my sights on making the Eastern Junior National Championship squad. The squad would represent the top juniors in the sport and would attend the Junior Nationals that were slated that year in Jackson Hole. I had made improvements in my training and was investing in a lot more hours of training that were paying off. And I made it.

I had a good race that day at the Putney School and finished fourth in the Eastern Championships.

I Almost Made it

Honestly, too, I was the recipient of a masterful wax job by my coach. Making the team in March of 1970 was, up till then, the greatest thrill of my young life. My loving parents were with me when I was named to the team at the Latchis Hotel in Brattleboro, Vermont. It was a watershed moment in my life. Looking back, I think they were more concerned about me making the team than I was. Or better put, how I would handle the disappointment of not making the team.

A lot of it wasn't totally fun, I must admit. Truthfully, too—and I don't think it that unusual—I was also motivated to be a decent athlete in order to attract girls. I loved them and wanted a girlfriend in high school, but I didn't have much luck. Even today, I don't understand why I didn't. Virtually no one seemed interested in me. Maybe I was a nerd. I sure was friendly enough, but I almost had to beg for a date to the junior and senior proms. It was enormously isolating. I remember going to school "make-out" parties where everyone would go upstairs at somebody's house, and I sat alone in the living room. One guy referred to me as the "peanut man" because I was the only one not paired off. It struck me as cruel, and I never forgot it. One nice thing did happen as I went off to college. I had plenty of dates and several serious relationships. But one girl from Illinois broke my heart. I really loved her, inasmuch as a nineteen-year-old can love. She was my absolute, knockout dreamboat. I think of her still. And what might have been.

So, within the week, the Eastern team was bound for Bozeman for some tune-up races at altitude and then to championships in Jackson Hole. It marked my first time going out West, and the first time on an airplane.

With the nation's top junior Nordic talent, I felt over my head right from the start. My races there proved nothing special, but I felt like just being there was a sort of victory, which I still hold true today. I reveled in the experience and the chance to get to better know my Eastern teammates, like Tim Caldwell, Scotty Broomhall, Rick Hale, Mike Guyer, and Ed Waters. The legendary jumper, Art Tokle, and Steve Williams served as our coaches. They were great and kind and helped manage us unruly boys with both discipline and grace.

Shortly after the Junior Nationals in 1970 were completed, I traveled to Inuvik, in Canada's Northwest Territories and above the Arctic Circle. I traveled with Bob Gray, Martha Rockwell, and a very young Jim Galanes, who was already showing tremendous potential then as a combined skier.

Traveling above the Arctic Circle required two

I Almost Made it

days of flying, including an overnight in Edmonton. Upon arrival I looked at the terrain and it was largely flat, not the rolling courses with ample climbing I was accustomed to. It was windswept with little tree cover, just stunted pine. Up there, the permafrost was a year-round phenomenon, and it was a biting, piercing cold that I'd never felt before. Most of the population of this small hamlet were made up of people of the Inuit First Peoples nation, and most of the Canadian national team called Inuvik home, thanks to a newly developed program called TEST. Territorial Experimental Ski Training was supported with funding from the Canadian government and run by the late Bjorger Pettersen (a Norwegian native who later would go on to oversee cross-country for the 1988 Olympic Winter Games in Calgary) and the charming Father J.M. Mouchet.

The local skiers were strong and already on the Canadian National Team. Fine skiers like Sharon and Shirley Firth, Roger Allan, and Fred Kelly, among others. At the end of Pettersen's coaching career, he had developed at least twenty-three athletes who went on to become national-team skiers. In fact, Sharon and Shirley were the first female indigenous athletes to compete for Canada in the Winter Olympics. Together, the twins earned a total of seventy-nine medals at various Canadian championships. Later, coach Pettersen remarked about them, "They didn't have an easy upbringing and were very timid when they first came to me. Of all the skiers I had, they were the most competitive and determined. In Inuvik we often skied when it was forty below zero; their lungs were used to the cold weather." Later, Sharon went on to be rewarded by being named to the prestigious Member of the Order of Canada.

The trip was long, and daunting, but it was a tremendous experience and I got to race against all of Canada's best, such as Oddvar Braa of Norway. It was an eye-opener and also confirmed that I wanted to really commit to the sport in a big way. I was certain then that I wanted to ski race in college. The only problem was my less-than-average grades in high school. I was probably about a C student through most of high school, more committed to sport and skiing than to homework. I tested poorly and my math scores were probably at about a sixth-grade level when I graduated in June of 1970. In truth, I'm certain now I would have been diagnosed with ADD or ADHD, but no one spoke of that then, and I had next to no help from the school's guidance counselor, which left me very much on my own to ferret things out. Even then, my parents couldn't help me out much.

I Almost Made it

During my senior year I was highly recruited by UVM, Bates, St Lawrence, and Dartmouth, none of which I could ever be admitted to with my low grades and scores. So I looked to the West, where two programs interested me: Fort Lewis and Western State, both in Colorado. I may not have been as skilled as others, but I had lofty goals and I wasn't afraid of hard work. But I was always nervous racing. I'd throw up before races, or not sleep well, or talk in my sleep (I'm told), or have anxious dreams. Already I had my doubts about this stuff, and it seemed my racing was an epic struggle for success and to prove myself and my worth. The better I got, the more the nerves were dancing upon me. Even then it seemed that every race was like a struggle for survival. It's not the best way to perform.

I had met the Fort Lewis coach, Dolph Kuss, at the 1970 NCAA skiing championships, liked him immediately, and loved the camaraderie I saw with the likes of Jimmy and Pat Miller of Maine, and Mike Scott, a Southern Vermont boy like me, from Rutland. It was decided, and I couldn't wait to travel to Durango and wear the classy yellow-and-blue racing suits of FLC. Fort Lewis had a very strong team and I was delighted to be a part of it. They were made up of fine skiers—Alpine and Nordic from around the country—and I liked them all.

FORT LEWIS

4

After graduating in 1970, I traveled out to Durango, Colorado, to begin my fledging racing career at Fort Lewis College. Our coach, Dolph Kuss, had impressive credentials and had been a two-time Olympic coach, and I was again lucky to have him.

Durango, located in the Four Corners region of Southwest Colorado, is an alluring and picturesque area, a town that for a long time held onto its real Western roots. I loved it the moment I saw it. It was and still is a real cowboy town—and who doesn't like a little cowboy? First stop in Durango after checking in was to the famed Hogan's Store, where Mickey styled me in a Western hat and boots. I couldn't wait to return to my somewhat Ivy League roots in Vermont to show off! What's more, long before the days of today's remarkable microbrews, I would drive back home with four cases of Coors beer—unavailable in the East—and my friends loved it. It felt cool.

The team Dolph had assembled was nearly world class. I was surrounded by a number of the best juniors in the nation, as well as recently graduated US Olympians like Mike Elliott, Mike Devecka, and Jimmy and Pat Miller.

The workouts there under Coach Kuss were as hard and demanding as anything I had ever done. His mantra was that our training didn't start when we arrived in September, but rather continued. You needed to show up fit, and lord help you if you didn't, for Dolph knew a great deal about physical training and the strength required for XC skiing. We trained six days a week, and quickly I started to get really fit.

The workouts replicated National Team training camps, as Dolph was still the head coach of Nordic combined for the USA, and he went to work not only training us college boys but his national team charges too. Dolph's son, Sepp, is now one of the world's greatest road cyclists, especially adept at climbing.

I Almost Made it

About one week into my freshman year at FLC, Dolph and Mike Elliott arranged for a training camp at high altitude in the San Juan mountains between Durango and Silverton. Most of us on the hike had precious little experience in backpacking and it must have shown. Long before high-tech fabrics were de rigueur, most of us brought ample supplies of cotton T-shirts, running shorts, a pair of jeans, and little else. Dolph supplied the tents and equipment essentials like sleeping bags and food.

The first few days were simply spectacular, as the early autumnal colors were starting to display their magic. There was heavy speed hiking along with some spectacular trout fishing in isolated mountain lakes. For me to be surrounded again by my heroes was indeed magical, and I was really enjoying this new world.

And then it started to snow. At first, beautiful light flakes swirled, later a powerful snowstorm, most of us experiencing our first hike in the mountains without the proper clothes or footwear.

At first it was funny. Noting the irony of being in the mountains, with it snowing, and we so unprepared. The tent my teammate Joe Bristol and I had set the night before was now awash with water, as the rain and then the snow ran under it with wild abandon. Then we were completely soaked to the skin. Everything—and I mean everything—was drenched, and the temperature was dropping rapidly. That night I had to share a dry bag with Mike Elliott, which was a life saver, and for years that night became the stuff of locker room legend.

The next morning we hiked out of the San Juan's to Silverton on the final leg of our trip, covering well over thirty miles that day. I felt tested to the max, but also immensely proud that I had managed to keep up. It was a lesson in pure toughness and grit that has never left me. Still, it was hard won, and was simply a preview of the kind of lessons I would learn at the Fort.

My four years in Durango were tough but also great. I improved my strength, my fitness, and my racing skills, and by my junior year I was able to break into the top ten at a number of RMISA carnivals. I figured that was about the best I could do, and never really committed to an Olympic team; yet I lived it closely through my teammates who were Olympic team members, especially in 1972 and 1976.

I wasn't a great student in high school, nor was I one in college. I was so fixated on skiing and its culture and the bonds of comradeship that it prompted my highly educated father, Van, to say repeatedly the only book I ever read was John

I Almost Made it

Caldwell's Cross-Country Ski Book. Frankly, he was nearly right. Now I am a voracious reader and am a person compelled to learn more. My literary tastes now run from the daily New York Times to the New Yorker, and loads of nonfiction books that my ex-wife teases me about, noting wryly, "Can't you ever read fiction?" The answer is, sadly, no.

It was also at Fort Lewis that I started broadcasting, which continued to catch my fancy, first at the new college radio station and later calling KIUP Radio in Durango with reports on the ski team's success on the RMISA College Carnival circuit. The broadcasting, however small, stirred something in me. I'd race, and at the conclusion of the weekend, I'd call KIUP with a voice report on the results. I liked doing it immediately. The weekly reports were well received in the Durango market. It was my debut on radio and I wanted to do more of it. So after the first year of doing this, I was asked to join the late Ted Foster, the station manager, in co-commentary of Fort Lewis College football. I saw that so much of this was interconnected.

While at FLC, I made many friends and loved the robust college party scene, on what must certainly be one of the world's most majestic college campuses, rimmed by the ramparts of the San Juan Mountains. A place, too, where snow came early.

I grew my flaming red hair to shoulder length and partied with the best of them. Spring days drinking 3.2% beer along with the consumption of pot passed by all too quickly . . . sometimes in a haze. God, they were good times. Sipping the nectar of Coors beer high in the Rockies seemed so sublime and hip. Of course, this era also paralleled the growing popularity of singer John Denver, whom many of us, I suppose, tried to emulate in looks, with wire-rim glasses and down vests. Looking back, it was all harmless and a sweet display of Rocky Mountain tribalism.

I fell in and out of love several times, and I began to learn some hard-won lessons in life. I would get married right after graduating, not heeding my parents' advice to go slowly, which would prove to be a hard learning experience. Just too young. I was so sure I was right. What a beauty and all-around lovely person Lynn was. She became my rock my senior year in college. She loved art and loved the simple things in life, loved to bake and create, and I fell madly in love with her.

In 1974, my senior year, I qualified to ski in the NCAA Skiing Championships held in Jackson Hole, Wyoming. It was my one and only time skiing in the Championships and my expectations were high. I'd had a pretty good year and was hoping

I Almost Made it

to end my skiing career on a high note. Sadly, I did not. I skied well in the first college team relay, where we were third, but my individual race was held on very wet, soft snow, klister-wax conditions. I had almost always a preference for skiing in cold, hard-packed snow. It was a bright, sunny day and there I saw two Norwegian athletes that skied for Denver University and Wyoming unveil the first of the brand-new fiberglass skis that were first used a few weeks before in the 1974 World Nordic Championships in Falun, Sweden. Most of the rest of the field were still using wooden skis. I was witnessing the end of the wooden-ski era, and a dramatic shift that seemingly happened overnight. Of course, the switch was to change waxing forever, too. The beloved scent of pine tar—redolent of a pine forest, which we burned to the base of the skis with torches—would be gone forever.

I think I finished among the top thirty or so, but I honestly can't recall now. I was disappointed with my showing, and knowing that it was likely my last serious race, I was somewhat heartbroken. But it made my decision to end racing easier. I had done my best, but it wasn't close enough. I suppose those results helped me to wrap up racing, which I adored, but I was never going to be an Olympian or US Ski Team member, I reasoned. I knew I wanted to stay involved in ski racing, so I hung up the skis for another growing interest of mine: the world of broadcasting. By that time, I had a growing confidence in my storytelling prowess, my baritone voice, and my knowledge of the sport.

DURANGO BROADCASTING BLASTOFF

5

Armed with some newly required announcing background—there were no broadcast journalism courses at Fort Lewis then—I learned through the school of hard knocks. Sometimes the best teacher.

Right after my graduation in 1975, I pestered the late Ted Foster until he gave me a full-time job, that of News Director of KIUP/KRSJ, the local station where I had done football broadcasts, as well as my ski-racing reports. Ted knew I was aggressive and had a good voice for delivery, and it didn't take much convincing.

I anchored the morning news, the noon block, and the five o'clock news program, and I scoured the local scene for news. I was a young hotshot. One time I remember a developing story was happening around Pagosa Springs. It was reported that a group of people—later to include many of the Heavens Gate devotees who took their own lives in California—were going to launch out of a rocket ship. I had gotten a tip that they were all riding in a van decorated with a sign that read "Space Fetus," and so I staked out the Pagosa area in our news van. I followed them into Durango and they proved to be a band booked to play Durango's Holiday Inn.

I interviewed many of the large names that came to Durango to perform, from Jerry Lewis to Tammi Wynette and CW McCall, who penned the CB radio song, "Convoy." There were perp walks from the sheriff's office to court, and a dastardly fire that claimed two lives. I stayed remarkably busy getting all the stories from the Four Corners region. CB radios were all the rage and I had one, plus a police/sheriff and fire department scanner.

We were an affiliate of the Mutual Broadcasting System, and several times I submitted reporting that aired nationally on their hourly newscasts. "How cool is that?" I thought. I was also submitting regular news and sports features to several of the Denver powerhouse stations Like KOA Radio in Denver and Action7 News in New Mexico. My enthusiasm for this kind of work was at an all-time high. Looking back I was just priming the pump for what would happen later in my career.

It was intoxicating to see my stories on TV, and I was a version of Vlad the Impaler when chasing them. I loved the challenge of breaking news in the region. Stories had to be fettered out, and there were no cell phones or computers. We were in the Dark Ages of broadcasting. It wasn't much of an adjustment from ski racing, really. In radio you needed to be prepared with all the right gear to go live from the news van, and you needed to be aggressive. The adrenaline rush was similar. I think those traits were really transferable.

My new wife, Lynn, was from Southern California, and during the trips we made out there as newlyweds, I pestered major-market news directors, including at outlets like KNBC and KABC TV, with my résumé and tapes—even walking directly up to LA local-news star Kelly Lange at Magic Mountain to ask her for a job. Give me an A for effort. Most certainly I was lacking in experience and far too young to get a job at places like that, but at the time I just didn't see it. She was, to say the least, not impressed by my tactics.

At KIUP/KRSJ, I went after big Durango and regional stories with my trusty police scanner in my car and the ever-present tape recorder. It was a tight broadcast, and I recruited just about everybody at the station to voice reports, with lots of actualities to make it seem we had many reporters out in the field. My vision of the news was to make it seem big, and I was especially influenced by CKLW 20/20 News, which was based in Windsor, Ontario, and also Detroit. I used to hear them broadcast on my many trips driving across the country from Vermont to Colorado. It was blood-and-guts news at its finest (something Durango didn't need and wasn't ready for).

Regardless, I made an impact of sorts pretty quickly. It was all pretty heady stuff to me. I was on the air and loving it. It all made me feel like my work made me matter.

Then skiing came calling again. In the Fall of 1977, I was offered the PR job for the US Ski Team in Utah. How could I refuse? Still, I didn't know what was in store for me and my fledging career. Head first, I plunged in (again).

It was a move that quickly I would come to regret. And looking back, I see that as the first huge mistake I would make in not cutting my radio chops for another year or two. As noted, I had also become a freelance news reporter and shooter (film days, folks) for KOA Radio and Action 7

News in New Mexico. They liked my work and offered me a full-time job, twice, and both times I ultimately turned it down. Big mistake number two, duly noted. Even now, I wonder what my career path might have been like if I had taken the job as a sports reporter in New Mexico. Then, many people used that market to springboard quickly to LA, people like Dr. George Fishback, the colorful weatherman who left the market for a starring role as a weatherman at KABC TV.

The story is, apparently, that when hired by the US Ski Team, I was not fully vetted by key trustees of the team, and while we moved to Park City and I hit the ground running, as was my way, there were among them folks not pleased that I had been hired. Apparently I was too "Nordic" for them. Within a matter of weeks, I was fired and deeply perplexed about my next move.

I'd received my notice while driving Brad Briggs, a longtime USST Board member, down to the Salt Lake City airport. He delivered the bad news. Honestly, I was crushed, and like many things of that nature, it wasn't handled especially well. It was a huge blow to my self-esteem, and I struggled to make sense of it. How could they? It wasn't the last time I was displeased with the treatment I received by the US Ski Team. I felt deeply hurt, and it took me a long time to get over the bitterness. I was working without a net.

Then, as if taking pity upon me, the Nordic Program Director of the US Ski Team, John Bower, told me on my last day about a guy named Tony Wise. Tony was the owner of the Telemark Lodge in the northwoods of Wisconsin, in the tiny town of Cable. Tony, it seemed, had just started a race called the American Birkebeiner and was anxious to fill a Public Relations Director spot at the lodge. I simply had to be brave and suck it up. I called Tony and was hired sight unseen. Lynn and I packed up our Volvo wagon again, and a car her parents had given her, and left our apartment that we had recently leased. We took a right at Kimball Junction, and through tears, didn't look back. We were in Park City less than one month. Ouch.

ANOTHER MOVE, THIS TIME TO TELEMARK

6

My heart sunk as we tooled out of Utah. We were about to venture into the great unknown. Lynn was from Southern California and I was worried for her happiness. She was unsure, as was I, about the move. I felt terribly sorry for the situation I had placed her in, and I suppose that caused the first of several cracks that would lead to the end of our union after only two years. We didn't stand a chance. Now, I can look back and note that life doesn't often track along a linear course. There are many moments where things are not buttoned up and you just have to take a chance and be brave. I suppose that is where human growth comes from.

The drive to the Midwest took a few days and afforded both of us the time to ponder what it was that we were getting into. I recall arriving in the city of Minneapolis and seeing the large IDS tower and then driving north, quickly leaving the urbane Twin Cities for what seemed like hours of driving through America's flat heartland and miles and miles of pine forests.

When we arrived in the tiny hamlet of Cable, Wisconsin, I felt like I was near the end of the earth. Then, we arrived at Telemark Lodge.

It was a large, sprawling place that looked attractive and had a large fireplace. Tony Wise greeted us there and good-naturedly welcomed us to his lovely resort in the forest. The place boasted golf, tennis, four-star dining, lots of excellent cross-country skiing, and a modest Alpine ski area known as Mount Telemark. The legendary Billy Kidd of Winter Olympic medal fame once quipped that the fireplace at Telemark was taller than the small Alpine ski hill.

Telemark also featured truly fine dining; a fly-in fly-out airport, often used by Upper Midwest folks for the extraordinary Sunday brunch; and, of course, skiing on the weekends. Or a round of golf in the land of the Pines. Tony loved music too. All kinds. We featured people like Ricky Nelson, Ronny

I Almost Made It

Milsap, and Duke Ellington, along with jazz-great Earl "Fatha" Hines.

Lynn and I quickly searched for a place to live and found a charming, small log cabin on picturesque Lake Owen, lovely in August, brutal in December. We were there in a blinding snowstorm watching KDAL TV the night the Edmund Fitzgerald went down, and as the hours passed on, I recall thinking how terrible it must have been that night on Lake Superior.

Officially I stayed on four months in Tony's employ. I loved working for Tony but longed to be in a bigger population center. Cable was probably less than four hundred people, and in many respects it felt like the end of the road. Tony and I would remain friends, and he often hired me as an announcer. I left on the best possible terms.

I really cared for Tony and was inspired by his creativity and passion. To be sure, he was a genius. What a teacher he was for me. In my entire life, I never met a man quite like him. Tony's impact on the sport of Nordic skiing was enormous. He would be over one hundred years old now, and he influenced and encouraged me in ways that helped make me willing to dare, and that is truly not a great strength of mine. It may appear that way, but it's not.

Tony, really, can be credited with hosting the first FIS World Cup in cross-country skiing, and of course, the blockbuster success that was, and is, the American Birkebeiner. His fertile mind also gave birth to the World Loppet League. Nothing was off limits to try, so he encouraged us to think big. Tony did things first class; for him there was no other way. The banquets during the World Cup were lavish, and included a lot of Native American entertainment including some extraordinary drumming. Tony spent his life in skiing, even helping lay out the trails for Lake Placid's 1932 Olympic Winter Games, and spoke five language including Cree. He was one of the sport's leading personalities, and who could still stand on his hands when he gave a welcoming speech. My interview with him for ESPN was a highlight of my work. His piercing blue eyes were still full of life and wonder even at his advanced age.

I recall Tony asking me about passing a peace pipe around the room, to all the athletes as well. I told him they will never smoke on it, as they were always trying to avoid colds and the flu. So, in typical Tony style, he said, "I have got an idea. We'll put cigarettes in reed baskets and pass them around." It was quite a sight, seeing those elite athletes light up some cigs. I had to laugh. Somewhere there must be pictures.

I Almost Made it

Watching Tony grow old following his bankruptcy was not easy, as he longed for a return to those adrenaline-fueled days that would never come. My dear friend, Tom Kelly, who took my public relations position at Telemark after I left, was also profoundly influenced by Tony. Tom was so good to him and as loyal as the days are long. He was to make certain that when Tony passed on that he would have a special funeral service with Dixie Land jazz bands and a horse-drawn carriage bearing Tony's homemade pine casket. It was all deeply touching and a moving tribute to the legacy of an amazing personality.

Tony gave me a real start at public-address announcing by having me do the Birkie (the American Birkebeiner) and the early World Cups, known as the Gitchi Gami Games. Those were the first FIS World Cups for cross-country skiing. Tony even brought the legendary 114-year-old Herman Smith "Jackrabbit" Johannsen to Telemark for the races and the Birkie.

I had done some PA announcing in college, and even in my hometown doing American Legion baseball. It was really where I got my start. It's the loudspeaker at games, announcing starting lineups and calling the plays, including playing a little music. It was good training for finding your voice, learning the art of inflections and being "on air." It was good training. In fact, it's such good training that I think that many young PA announcers try to use it to springboard into television.

And off and on, I have continued to announce at the Birkie till this day. I still recall announcing the Birkie the year the pack of racers left the start about fifteen minutes early. There were a ton of Norwegians who traveled to ski the 55km race, and that tradition continued for many years. Here was the FIS technical delegate, the late Lars Kindem, and I with a wireless microphone, only feet away from the front line—and they were itching to go. As I recall it, Kindem then yelled, "Five minutes to start!" which many in the first wave didn't really understand, and in five seconds they were off like winter race horses. I never ran so fast in my life to get to the sidelines to avoid being swallowed up in a mass start of about fifteen thousand eager skiers. Lars and I were lucky to have avoided a major collision.

Still, another year's funny moment was when the actual winner coming into Hayward's Historyland finish line was completely unknown to us in the announcing booth. I kept trying to find the right words to say, even though Tom Kelly and I had no idea. So I kept saying the name of a previous winner, who was also in the lead pack: "Norwegian Bjorn Arvnes is among the leaders," I intoned. But

I Almost Made it

at the finish we had no name. The skier was a late entry taken late the night before, and he would nip Arvnes in the final kilometer. It was rather embarrassing. Later, we found the mystery winner was another Norwegian star, the young Arnt Harstead. He registered late and thusly was not on any start list.

At Telemark one year doing the Birkie, I was introduced to a man about my age from Duluth named Scott Keenan. He's also over time become a close friend. He had, the year before, started a marathon-running race along the shores of Lake Superior. It was known as Grandma's Marathon, for a popular Minnesota restaurant chain. "I'm looking for an announcer to do my race next June. Would you be interested?" Keenan asked me. I must have passed the audition, as he invited me the next summer to be the voice of his race.

Now, some forty-six years later of calling his race, I still return to Duluth every year. It's truly one of the highlights of my year. I've always loved Minnesota, especially the Northern Country and the Iron Range, and its accessibility to the famed Boundary Waters Canoe area, which my friend Gary Larson opened my eyes to. Pristine lakes full of fish, peaceful campfires, and the smell of the pines. I made many trips there and I was the richer for the experience, and I loved the people who were outdoors folk. When it came to Grandma's Marathon, I never felt a place that seemed closer to home, and I always felt the love and kindness of the Minnesota Nice folk; it's a real thing and it's a true treasure. I feel blessed.

Keenan was a natural-born promoter and turned Grandma's Marathon into a world-class event, complete with a hugely talented international field. It's now about the tenth-largest marathon in the country, and I've been lucky to grow old with it. Every year, I have the best seat in the house at the finish, and I love the energy of calling all the runners in. Scott, and all the other folks in the race, along with my longtime broadcast partner Mike Pinocci, a former national-class runner, have become real friends. Over the years, Mike and his wife, Kitty, and I have become good friends, and I think he is one of the best running announcers out there. Always prepared and humble, he connects with people, and I'm proud of the body of work we did together. Getting to know people connected to the race like Kevin Pates (a standout writer), Dick Beardsley, and many others has been a blessing, and I appreciate the insight into distance running they have shared freely with me. I have run two marathons, Grandma's and Twin Cities, in both

I Almost Made it

cases a shade over four hours— nothing to brag about, but I did have some satisfaction in doing them. And I'm proud to call them my own. They aren't easy.

Looking back, I see that I was able to weld my love of both skiing and broadcasting into a reasonable package of steady work. At Telemark, I was able to use all of my developing skills, from announcing the Birkie to the Lumberjack World Championships, nationally televised on ABC Sports. Heck, I even announced fireworks. I loved it all, and soon my career would have me pointed towards Minneapolis. One needs to stay open to opportunities that continue to move you forward in human growth and greater potential.

NORTUR DAZE & THE PHONE CALL

7

While working at Telemark, I crossed paths with a Norwegian living in Minneapolis who had recently started importing cross-country skis and equipment made in Norway. His name was Finn Haug, and we hit it off very well. With some financial help from the Norwegian Export Council, he was wholesaling ski brands including Epoke and Landsem, and Swix wax, among the better-known brands.

I was very fortunate to be hired by Finn as NorTur's Public Relations Director. He took a chance on me and it paid off for both of us. I quickly worked hard on a bevy of promotions, press releases, and sponsored events. All the things

I learned from Tony I was able to apply here. Here I was still dreaming big dreams.

Lynn and I quickly snagged a modest apartment in suburban Plymouth, Minnesota, and once again began the process of trying to stabilize our still-newly married life. Three homes in less than a year was very challenging for my new wife, and I always felt very much to blame for dragging her around the country as I searched for some manner of job stability. To this day it still pains me. She was a good person that deserved better. We divorced not long after arriving in Minneapolis. We were, in fact, married about two years, and we were far too young. From a distance now, I realize how selfish my job pursuits were. Strangely, I don't even think I asked Lynn, who passed away not so long ago, if she agreed with all the moving. I'm happy she remarried and had a wonderful family.

Working with a bunch of (mostly) like-minded guys as NorTur, we had a ball. I worked on sponsorship deals with the Birkie, the Epoke Cup Series, athletes on the US Ski Team, and adventurer and 1968 US Olympian Ned Gillette, who would take our gear on countless high-profile expeditions. The annual SIA show in Las Vegas was a huge deal. Famous skiers, selling skis, and digging all the hospitality suites at the Vegas Hilton. It was all bigger than life.

I Almost Made it

We even held a sand skiing race at Redondo Beach in California, and dubbed it the World Championships of Sand Skiing. We held a press conference at the LA Press Club and brought Birkie-winner Bjorn Arvnes over to compete. It was a hoot. Being held in the LA area, the entertainment capital of the world, it led me to do other things in television, including being a guest of the *Dinah!* (Shore) talk show, where I skied on Miami Beach with actor Anthony Quinn and country music star Eddie Rabbit. Without being too egotistical, my stock as a Nordic go-to person was on the rise.

I enjoyed my friendship with Ned Gillette, a fellow Vermonter, who was brilliant and funny as hell. Ned and I traveled around the country for a couple of years doing Norwegian Ski Council cross-country clinics, and he was not only extraordinarily brilliant, but a helluva fun guy to hang out with. He knew how to have a good time.

Around the same time, Tom Kelly and I started a travel tourism firm called Worldwide Nordic that would take people on guided tours to all the World Loppett races, which Tony had created. It was really among my first trips overseas, and we had a ball. Almost always it either started or ended in Munich, where there was an obligatory visit with all our guests to the famed Hofbräuhaus, a beer hall very popular with tourists. This became a highlight and the stuff of legend. It was a heady time, and we didn't make a lot of money, but it helped shape us and our love of European traveling. One time I scoffed five liters of their golden pils with our guests.

I was in my office at NorTur in Minneapolis one gloomy December day when our secretary Marlene Anderson patched a call into me from ABC Sports in New York. It was from Sports Vice President Chuck Howard. Howard told me they were looking for a Nordic announcer for the 1980 Winter Olympic games in Lake Placid, and asked if I was interested. You've heard of a New York minute . . . well, I responded yes in a New York millisecond.

ABC & MY FIRST OLYMPIC GAMES

8

What keeps us alive, what allows us to endure?
I think it is the hope of loving,
Or being loved.

—Meister Eckhart

I grew up idolizing ABC Sports. My dad and I watched Alpine skiing with Bob Beattie and Frank Gifford and ski jumping with Art Devlin on our black-and-white TV. It transported us not only to events like Kitzbühel or the Four Hills Tournee, but also to the coffee and pastry shops of Innsbruck. The storytelling was captivating, and I long dreamed that someday I'd be a part of it all. My old high school chum Craig Sweet and I would ride the T bar at Prospect Mountain and pretend to be those announcers calling the action from far flung—and only imagined—winter Alps. It stoked dreams in my young mind.

That day on the phone, Chuck Howard asked me to fly to New York for an interview, and I did. My then-girlfriend and soon-to-be-second wife, Jody, met me in New York at the Hilton, where I walked across the street to the ABC Television headquarters at 1330 Avenue of the Americas. Up to the 26th floor and soon I was meeting with Chuck Howard and the legendary Roone Arledge, President of ABC Sports and the man credited with really creating the template and model of TV coverage of the modern Olympic Games. Arledge was a hugely well-known figure in sports production, and I was in awe of him. And, I was scared shitless. The only way through this was to be both bold and brave.

The meeting lasted all of twenty minutes. They told me what they wanted me to do and what was expected of me. I floated out of the meeting, feeling on cloud nine and thinking I did well in the interview. Retreating to the Hilton, Jody and I shared an expensive scotch straight up. I was flirting with the big time, and didn't know enough to know what I didn't know about the Games. One of the biggest questions they wanted answered in my interview was, "did I know Bill Koch," and "did I have access to him." I said yes. Kochie, a fellow Vermont native, had taken a silver medal four years before in the 30km race at the 1976 Olympic Games in Innsbruck, and they were caught a bit off guard by it. This time they wanted to be ready. More on that later.

Then the ABC Sports lawyers started to prepare a contract and offered me a fee that required no negotiation. "How's ten thousand dollars sound for two weeks of work?" lawyer Bob Apter offered. I wasn't making much more at NorTur than that per year. So you bet I said that'll be just fine, smiling from ear to ear.

Then, in just a matter of weeks, I was off to Lake Placid. The anticipation was overwhelming, but I tried to keep it in check.

Working one's first Olympic Games is pretty heady stuff. Even then, it seemed bigger than life. The honest truth is that I really had no idea what to expect. I wondered if I could handle this gig in a manner befitting the glorious, forceful world that was ABC Sports. Perhaps I was also simply in awe of what was about to happen.

Jody and I tooled into the Hilton Hotel on Main Street in Lake Placid. The town was already jam-packed, brimming with anticipation and excitement. We opened the door to check in, and suddenly I realized my life would never be quite the same again.

Peter Graves

With a minimum of broadcaster experience, I wondered if I was an impostor here.

Of course, these were the days prior to the Internet, and finding information on the athletes was a huge task. Jody helped me research, and I was about as prepared as I could be for Games. Her steadying presence helped calm me. Good intelligence on athletes and storylines tended to be acquired through talking with people. I worked hard on cultivating sources and was lucky that I had the background of working in ski racing, especially with a Norwegian ski company, which helped a great deal in sourcing Scandinavian news.

There they were. The big guns of ABC Sports. There was Roone . . . "oh! McKay just walked by. There's Bob Beattie." Jody and I tried to whisper, hoping my feigning wouldn't be so obvious. But the real big shots on network TV sports were there.

Just being around the legendary nice guy Jim McKay and others like Frank Gifford and Don Meredith was a hoot. I loved it. "Dandy Don" and his wife shared a room next to ours at the Hilton, and we became quite good friends. He was very easygoing, just like you saw on Monday Night Football on ABC.

I got a package of ABC clothing for the "talent." It was like Christmas morning. Bags of ABC stuff,

I Almost Made it

and above all the true classic: the ABC Bogner parka for the on-air team. I still have it, though it ceased to fit decades ago.

I was really expecting to help get cross-country skiing and biathlon on the air. And I pushed like hell. But the coverage was small, about five minutes or so a day. I was infuriated and said so to several of my producers, not what they wanted to hear from a young and very green network journalist. Looking back, I don't think it served me well to make a fuss. I simply tried then to do my best each day and contribute where I could.

One thing I quickly sensed was that everyone played by a different set of rules, and these rules are ones you don't learn in the best journalism schools. It was up to me to see how this game was played. Some of the tech people, however talented, were in a chronic state of being pissed off, and despite that, I always tried to make nice. I was so thrilled and enthusiastic to be there and filled with a childish idealism that I was going to make things happen at the Games for my sports. I had a lot to learn.

I worked with the late Bill Fleming, who was a standout announcer normally assigned to college football telecasts. He was smooth and skilled, and seemed to have about zero interest in cross-country skiing. His goal, it appeared, was to get his face on the tube as often as possible. "Face time," they call it in the biz. Fleming, I feel certain, wanted a maximum of himself and a minimum of me. My producer, Ned Steckel, asked me quietly one day early on if I'd gotten the stiff arm from Fleming. I told him yes, quite literally, a stiff arm which indicated I'd talked enough and to shut it down. Out of deference, I obliged, but I'll never forget it, ever. It was intimidating.

Truth is, though I knew something of my sport, my experience was lacking and it was somewhat frightening. I never thought I was ready, but you don't turn an opportunity like that down. I was so engaged in the network-TV process that I learned a vast amount in Lake Placid. Firstly, I came to understand those commentators I had placed on high were just people, like everyone else. Sometimes I felt like there were few truly brave or intelligent voices among them, and it was much more important to have great hair, a nice chin line, or a thin waist. In my years doing TV, I have to reflect that its magic drew in among many of the most narcissistic, self-important people with unparalleled vanity that I have come across. But not all are that way, and there are many journalists out there who care about the story more than the shade with pancake makeup. Hey, I thought, I can

I Almost Made it

play this game. There's room for me. All and all it was truly captivating and I desperately wanted to be among the few that created the soundtrack to grand sporting events. It's a drug of sorts, a narcotic. Just look today at the thousands of young people that want to be among the anointed in network sports departments. It's like Icarus flying towards the sun.

So I awaited with apprehension that I would be put into an uncomfortable situation, and it didn't take long. The men's 30km at the Lake Placid Olympics was the first Nordic event, and the suits expected Kochie to medal again. Fleming and I were at Mount Van Hoevenberg to call the action.

Kochie started the race and expectations were high, but after some slow going he decided to drop out. This is not all that unusual, and the word was he wanted to save himself for the remainder of the Olympic program. Honestly, I understood and didn't think much about it. To me, it made perfect sense. But that's not what the network brass had in mind.

After we got out of the booth from calling the race, I was approached by my ABC Sports producer who said I had to interview Bill ASAP. I knew Bill pretty well, and always respected him as an athlete but also as a person. He was a visionary in the sport, helping later to popularize the skating technique, but he was soft spoken and had some well-earned distrust of the media in general. I always respected that. I told my producer I thought getting an interview on camera would be hard, and that I was uncomfortable invading his private space. "I don't care," said the producer, and what's more, this request came "right from the top." That meant Roone.

Now the pressure was mounting on me. There was no choice, I had to try. One of the coaches told me Kochie was still at the venue, so I went out behind the timing building to try and find him. "He'll be back, he's out cooling down. I think you'll find him." So along with me, on my first day at the Games, came a camera man, a sound guy, and a grip. I finally did spot Bill and explained privately the situation, and luckily for me he agreed to talk on camera. At that moment, I felt like Mike Wallace at 60 Minutes doing a stakeout. The camera rolled and I asked a few questions. It became a window into Bill's soul and his deeply held convictions. "Let's not talk about this race, let's talk about the human race," he said, and while the interview played that night during prime time, I never felt comfortable doing it. I always thought well of Bill to agree to do it.

I Almost Made it

The Olympics went on and things got easier. Fleming and I called the closest race in XC skiing history, the battle between Thomas Wassberg of Sweden and the giant Finn, Juha Mieto. It was a seminal moment in Nordic ski history. Afterwards, again hanging by the timing building with friends who were working inside, a nicely dressed gentleman came in with one other person. They were unknown to me. They carried champagne and fluted glassware. The man turned out to be the King of Sweden, who toasted the timers for their exacting precision. The race was won by one-one-thousandth of a second. It was a special moment to witness, and one I'll never forget.

Of course, the Miracle on Ice took center stage at those Games, where a talented bunch of truly amateur college kids bested the mighty Soviets at their own game.

The scene outside the Olympic area was extraordinary, with crowds cheering "USA, USA," and people spilling onto Main Street, hugging, kissing, and dancing. It was a night of joy and celebration that was truly affecting.

Then, as quickly as it began, ABC did their credit roll and went to black, Jim McKay working his usual mastery with grace and elegance. I took a deep breath. I had survived and done some solid reportage and perhaps even flourished under ABC training.

In May of 1980, on the heels of the Winter Olympics, I married my old high school girlfriend, Jody Roberts. She, for years, always had my back, which I am still undyingly grateful for, and the union produced two wonderful children in Katie and Willy Graves, whom we both adore. We were to be married for twenty-three years. My near-constant travel took a real toll on our union, for which I deeply regret. Yet, I continued to chase the brass ring.

My son Willy started ski jumping at five years old and took to it quickly, making rapid progress during the next decade. We first made a crude jump in our backyard off a rock. Willy was named to the US Ski team in the sport of Nordic combined, a complex discipline combing cross-country skiing and ski jumping. He skied on three US World Junior teams and traveled the world, and was close to making the 2010 Olympic team for Vancouver. Among his many outstanding performances was winning the national collegiate championships while a student at Salt Lake's Westminster College. Willy was a very determined athlete. He really embraced the sport. I am so proud of his many achievements.

I Almost Made It

My daughter, Kate, took to cross-country skiing like a natural and skied for four years on the Putney School team. It was also during that time she took to bike racing as well. Katie was good in both sports. Upon marrying Mark Bowen, the pair built their own house and had an extensive farming operation. Not long ago they traveled south to Tennessee, where they are building their own place. I am so proud of their ingenuity and work ethic. They have a child, my only grandson, James Bowen, who is an extraordinary hard worker.

They are a great joy to me. And I love being a father. My children are very close to my heart.

ESPN: THE EARLY DAYS

9

Armed with work for ABC Sports on my résumé, I sent several letters off to the fledging network ESPN in Connecticut. It was my friend Tom Kelly, always aligned with current media trends, who told me about the start of this new twenty-four-hour sports network. It was born in 1979 by Bill Rasmussen, a former PR man with the defunct Hartford Whalers. His goal was to cover UConn sports, but found being on the transponder gave him national access. The Entertainment and Sports Programming Network was born out of humble origins.

I guess nearly twenty-four hours later I had fired off a tape and a résumé. I was hired to do the fledgling network's ski program and to voice in Bristol as a host of FIS Nordic programming, often cast with the well-know announcer Jim Simpson. ESPN was in the process of being built when I did the first shows in the garage with a porta potty out front. Those were the early days of cable TV, and the atmosphere was energized and heady. I loved it. If ABC Sports was the pinnacle of sports TV, the early days at ESPN were refreshingly low key, with all the energy of a frat house. Making sports TV was fun and featured a deeply creative process. One producer gave me the ultimate compliment: "You see things others just don't see." Wowzer.

I did World Cups in ski jumping live with Jim Simpson from Lake Placid—while he was suffering from an untimely bout of Bell's Palsey—and scads of shows that I voiced-over solo in Bristol. The ESPN job would also bring me to two Olympic Winter Games, covering the Sarajevo Games in 1984 with George Grande in studio in Bristol, and the 1988 Calgary Olympic Games in a remote studio out of CFCN in Calgary. Those were exceptionally busy Games for me as I was the public address announcer during the day in Canmore for cross-country skiing, and then would drive down to Calgary for the evening Olympic show. This marked the first

I ALMOST MADE IT

Games in which I wore two parkas, one from the Organizing Committee and the other from ESPN, as both a metaphor and a reality. I was young, enthusiastic, and had plenty of energy and felt completely gratified by what I was doing.

In those early days in Bristol, some of the most used phrases were, "don't worry, will fix it in post," or, your mistake on air "gave the show a live feel." ESPN was just starting and I was in on the deal on the front end for once.

I worked the 1984 Sarajevo Games in Bristol and was paired with the true gentleman, George Grande, who was as pleasant as can be, and was always encouraging. Another great guy was Greg Gumble, who anchored the nightly show. Then I worked at the Calgary Games and traveled each night to Calgary to appear on our set show with the late John Saunders, who was also a lovely man. It was at these Games that the late Marty Hall, who was then coaching for the Canadian National XC team, let loose with some less than subtle comments implicating the Russians of using performance-enhancing drugs, which was mostly likely true. Marty had to bear the brunt of those comments, which were an honest reflection of what his gut was telling him. The Organizing Committee and Sport Canada was livid that a Canadian coach had made those comments. I admired the New Hampshire-born Hall for having the courage and bravery to speak up.

That day I walked into the press room at Canmore to see Hall being hammered by journos anxious to find the truth. Marty said to me: "Hey Gravey, don't stand too close, I'm Kryptonite, baby." Hall's comments had resonated deeply, but I wasn't ever going to throw him under the bus. "You're my friend, and I don't give a damn for the Hall haters, what you said needed to be said. This has likely been going on for years now and it's not fair. I'm proud of you." In truth, probably only someone like Marty, could have verbalized publicly what many other nation's trainers had been thinking. Plus, what was happening deeply affected Marty's superb Canadian star Pierre Harvey, who should have been the home team's superstar in cross-country skiing. Harvey retired not long after the '88 Olympic Games. And had become disillusioned about the use of PEDs in sport.

I spent about fifteen years doing shows for ESPN. It was a great run. Many of them were USSA televised events from cross-country to freestyle to ski jumping. I traveled the country. It was a real gift, and I really enjoyed interviewing athletes and coaches, and helping craft creative opens for the shows. I look back now and think, "Ya know, some of that was pretty darned good." I had always had a creative mind. Now it was paying off, displaying my signature "charm."

Then one fine day, it was over, simple as that.

I'll never forget the call from a coordinating producer for skiing at ESPN. It ended my hopes and dreams in a forty-five-second phone call. "We're going in a different direction," he said. Little did I realize at the time, that was (less than) coded language that my time there was up. No "great job," no thanks for the dedication, just the end. Honestly, it hurt like hell. I sank into a depression, and wondered why I was being replaced by someone else. Not necessarily someone better, just someone else. And someone, to some degree, I'd helped mentor.

Little did I know this scenario would play out many more times in my love-hate relationship with television sports. For others, in the fickle business of television sports, experience the same thing playing out time after time. There's no objective criteria to judge one's performances, just someone's gut feelings. Television, I reasoned, was not for the faint of heart. It's a cruel business at times, and especially for those "talent folks" whose work puts them in front of the camera. For many, a place for extraordinary ego fulfillment, for others, those blessed with telegenic looks. I started to see TV sports for many as a kind of narcotic, where the well had to be filled often. Having now done several Olympic Games and many shows already, I could see how "talent" worked it to get more on-air time. To watch this play out in its many forms was instructive and revealing. To survive in this at the network level, you needed to be rather hard boiled, tough, and willing to play the game. Fame was fleeting and everyone knew it. After all, it was just a phone call away.

Nice-guy sportscasters, for the most part, were relegated to small markets like Duluth, Burlington, or Manchester, NH. And there were some truly fine people there making use of the airwaves to tell inspiring stories and spreading good will through sport.

Still, my time working with ESPN was largely terrific. For me, it was always about the quality of my work, my interviews, and my writing; and I'm stilled filled with gratitude towards the remarkable people there, like Tom Reilly, Peter Englehart, George Grande, Boomer and Scotty Conall, Bill Fitts, and Chet Simmons. They were as nice to me as I could have ever hoped for. Men of a different era.

While there are many good announcers out there in TV Land, there are fewer still these days that rise to true greatness. I worked with a few of them, people like Jim McKay and Jack Whittaker. Especially McKay, who was equally brilliant as an announcer and as a human being. A newspaperman at first, he could eloquently and sparingly write brilliantly for television. His work heading up ABC Sports' compelling coverage of the Munich Olympic games tragedy—leading to the senseless slaughter of the Israeli athletes there—was among the most evocative moments ever recorded, and it was all live. He received an Emmy for his work covering the unfolding drama.

One of the nicest local guys I ever was honored to know was the long-time sports anchor at KDAL TV in Duluth, Marsh Nelson. He loved sports, loved the kids, and was one of the most decent, loving men I ever met. He loved TV, but didn't need it, and he had no ego. Watching him often reminded me that nice guys could finish first. He was one of them for sure. Grandma's Marathon gives out the annual Marsh Nelson award in his memory, and it goes to a local sports journalist who goes above and beyond in promoting the race.

Peter Graves racing for Fort Lewis College in 1971.

I Almost Made It

Graves racing at George Washington Birthday Race at Putney School in Vermont.

Peter and members of the Fort Lewis and US Nordic Combined Team at the start of the infamous hike into the San Juan, CO, wilderness—which turned into something of a survival mission—taken at the Narrow Gauge Railroad in Durango, CO. The Four Corners region was hit especially hard by a freak storm system, unusual for that time of year and we were well above 10,000 feet in rain and snow. In the lower elevations, twenty-three people died. Interestingly, more rain fell in nearby Arizona and Utah: 11.40 inches of rain fell during a 24-hour period that night of September 5, 1970. In the Four Corners region the damage was estimated to be in the area of nearly 3 million dollars. And we were right in the center of it all.

I Almost Made It

A backshot of Peter, racing for Mt. Anthony Union High School, at Prospect Mountain in Woodford, Vermont.

Peter working the 1988 Calgary Olympics for ESPN, along with the entire ESPN Calgary team. The set was constructed at CFCN TV in Calgary.

Peter and famed announcer Greg Lewis talk about the differences in skis at Copper Peak, outside of Ironwood, MI, during an FIS ski flying event for NBC's *SportsWorld*.

Peter and ABC veteran Bill Fleming before the start of an XC race at Lake Placid. Bill was one of the original announcers for ABC Sports.
PHOTO CREDIT: BOB WOODWARD.

Announcing at the American Birkebeiner in Wisconsin.
PHOTO CREDIT: TOM KELLY

A fledgling reporter for ESPN, Peter interviews Nordic skiing legend Herman Smith "Jackrabbit" Johannsen at Telemark Lodge in Wisconsin. Johannsen devoted much of his life to building trails and was a huge presence in the sport. He resided much of his life in Canada, and returned to Norway to pass at a remarkable 111 years of age. He returned to Quebec for burial and rests at the Saint Sauveur Cemetery in Quebec, next to his wife. His archives are held at McGill University in Montreal.
PHOTO CREDIT: JODY ROBERTS GRAVES

Peter delighted in interviewing Franz Klammer of Austria, the gold medalist in the Downhill from the Innsbruck Olympic Winter Games in 1976 for Jalbert Productions at their Celebrity Ski Week in Vail, CO.

In his first assignment for network television, Peter teamed up with the legendary Bill Fleming to cover cross country skiing and biathlon for ABC Sports in Lake Placid. In the middle was Vermont's Bill Koch who took a silver medal for the US four years before in Innsbruck, Austria.

PHOTO CREDIT: JODY ROBERTS GRAVES

At the Lake Placid Olympic Winter Games, outside the International Broadcast Center, Peter enjoys a chance to catch up with the famed Don Meredith, both on the ABC Sports team. Meredith was a long-time Dallas Cowboys quarterback, often referred to as "Dandy Don" (a name given to him by Howard Cosell during his long-stint as a commentator for ABC's Monday Night Football, where he appeared from 1970-1984 as part of the original cast). PHOTO CREDIT: BOB WOODWARD

Peter Graves

One of my many credentials for the 1980 Olympic Winter Games in Lake Placid.

(Below) Peter and Kjell-Erik Kristiansen working together in the broadcast booth during the 2011 FIS World Nordic Championships at Holmenkollen, Oslo, Norway. Graves, was the first American to announce at Holmenkollen.

Peter and World Champion Johnny Spillane ready to do our stand-up open at Lake Placid, NY, for World Cup Ski Jumping.

The first American to announce at Holmenkollen Ski Festival in Oslo, 2011.

John Caldwell shares a special moment with Peter at Craftsbury.

Peter Graves was elected to the US Ski and Snowboard Hall of Fame in March of 2023 for his lifetime work broadcasting for the sport. On the left is Graves' son, Willy, a former US Ski team member, and on the right, his lifelong friend, Tom Kelly.

I'm especially proud of one of my Harvard skiers, who has gone on to great things running races and serving as a TD, Ollie Burrass. I'd love to think I opened some doors to the joys of racing for him, and other Crimson skiers.

PHOTO: PETER GRAVES

Peter hosting cross-country skiing and ski jumping at the 2010 Olympic Games in Vancouver.

The announcing team for Alpine skiing at the 2018 Olympic Winter Games in Korea.

Announcing the US Nationals at Craftsbury, Vermont.
PHOTO CREDIT: REECE BROWN

I'm suffering from Bell's Palsy in an early ski jumping show for ESPN alongside famed announcer, Jim Simpson. Somehow, I pulled it off.

Picture of my mentor, John Caldwell, who was a member of the 1952 US Olympic Team in Oslo. This photo was taken in the Old Lake Placid 1980 Olympic stadium.

Hosting Alpine Skiing at the 2014 Olympic Games, Sochi Russia.

The 2024 FIS World Cup at Beaver Creek, Colorado, announcing team with World Championship medalist Doug Lewis and the legendary Daron Rahlves, winner of the fabled Hahnenkamm DK at Kitzbuhel, Austria, in 2003.

1992 OLYMPICS AT TNT

10

In late 1991, and with the knowledge that Turner Network Television (TNT) would be joining forces with CBS Sports in exercising the cable TV rights to the upcoming 1992 Olympic Winter Games in Albertville, France, I dropped a note to the Executive Producer at TNT, the late Mike Pearl. I was very interested in helping them out with their Nordic coverage of the Games. Pearl responded back quickly to let me know that they'd like to hire me for their telecasts. He sent me a contract, and I was thrilled that I would be working on the set in Atlanta with (the late) Nick Charles and Fred Hickman. I was thrilled to be doing another Olympic Games.

Peter Graves

Shortly thereafter, my airline ticket arrived and I was booked in an Atlanta Hotel near the studio. Then Pearl left Atlanta to be on-site in France to produce the daily show.

Prior to leaving, I received a call from a senior producer at Turner, a veteran of sports TV production, about what to expect. In Pearl's absence, he would be in charge in Atlanta. "Looking forward to having you," he said, and then he advised me to bring some blue shirts, which look better on camera.

I was thrilled, and jumped on the plane for Atlanta. When I got my bags, there was a huge, white stretch limo waiting for me outside, which brought me to the hotel to drop off bags and then to the TNT studios on Techwood Drive.

After some warm hellos, I met some of the folks I'd be working with. Shortly thereafter, the puzzled senior producer I'd spoken with approached me— and then my world collapsed. "I'm not exactly sure why you're here, and what exactly you're going to do. In the interim we hired another commentator, Brian Drebber, and he's already in France," he said. My hopes sank, and I was understandably confused. "I'm afraid we double-hired for this spot," he offered. A term I had never heard of before, but I'm guessing I'm not the only announcer this has ever happened to.

I was angry, confused, and it really hurt. I was so ready for the shows and had spent hours preparing for my role. I couldn't believe this was happening. I'd told so many people I'd be on air for TNT, and I felt ashamed and couldn't think fast enough on my feet to come up with a good answer without baring my soul. So, clearly, there was no role for me there, and after forty-eight hours, I limped onto the plane to fly back to Hartford. There was no limo ride this time to bring me to Atlanta's Hartsfield. I took a cab.

Looking back, I think I understand more clearly what occurred there. It is, frankly, part of the human condition. Nothing was done to me with malice; it just happened. Still, I have immense respect for the Olympic Games and their collective power, and I felt too easily dismissed. I dearly wanted to be involved, but it was a lesson learned and a perspective gained. Yeah, shit happens. When I got back to my home, I cried my eyes out, bitter tears of profound sadness.

In fact, this did have a rather devastating effect on me personally. I tried and failed to get hired for the glorious games of 1994 in Lillehammer, and the 1998 Games in Nagano. It was a long stretch without the dreams of the Olympics, but I did find work announcing skiing for OLN TV, CTV in Canada, and a host of public-address events like the

US Nationals, both Alpine and Nordic. And I was doing a great deal of mountain-bike announcing for ESPN during this time, which was booming. For that I traveled a great deal during this period all over the world.

In 1988 I was asked by my friend Brian Stickel to announce what was becoming the popular sport of mountain biking. There was a NORBA National Series, and countless UCI World Cups that took me around the world. They were busy weekends, as I was also hosting shows for both ESPN and OLN, but my very first race was near my home at Mount Snow, Vermont. I loved it immediately. It was tribal like skiing and surfing and I felt I fit right in. I traveled to Capetown, South Africa, as well as Japan, France, Germany, Austria, New Zealand, and Australia, just to mention a few. It elevated my profile to the point that I did many World Championships and two Summer Olympic Games.

In Australia, I enjoyed one of the thrills of my lifetime, traveling twice to the fabled Great Barrier reef for diving, and witnessed a kaleidoscope of coral and fish of every color. It took my breath away. Both of those trips occurred when we were racing in Cairns, a magical tropical rainforest of a course. All of these sports helped me spread my wings professionally.

I Almost Made it

With the Olympics coming up in 2000 in Sydney, I scored a hire as one of the announcers for the mountain-bike venue, which was a resounding success and a boost for my ego. They were marvelous Games, the people open and friendly.

The next few years I spent freelancing, working with OLN and the Special Olympics, and also keeping up my PA-announcing work at Grandma's Marathon and my longtime gig at Beaver Creek for the FIS Alpine World Cup, including two World Championship events there. The people at the Vail Valley Foundation have been wonderful to me from the start. Since the start at Beaver Creek, and later at the wonderful World Cup in Killington, I have been teamed with my friend Doug Lewis, who is a great commentator. We fit together very nicely. It's hard to believe, but Doug and I have worked together now some thirty years.

SALT LAKE CITY

11

There is more hunger for love and appreciation in this world than for bread.

—Mother Teresa

In the late Summer of 2000, I was approached by the Salt Lake Olympic Organizing Committee about taking a job as the lead snow-sports producer for the 2002 Olympic Games. It was a video conference call that I did in Brattleboro.

Apparently, I did well enough, and had considerable background by then to get the job. Shortly after the Summer Olympic Games, where I announced mountain biking, I moved out to Salt Lake with the full support of my then-wife. I was not only going to do plenty of PA announcing at the Games, but I would also play a collaborative role in helping hire and vet other announcers for all the Olympic venues.

The two-year experience was a fantastic one, and I'll never forget it. I rented a small room in a house belonging to friends and worked on making recommendations for the hiring of venue public-address announcers for each sport. My boss was a talented young woman named Christy Nicolay, who had come from the world of extreme sports, like ESPN's X Games and the Gravity Games. She was smart, creative, and we worked very well together. For me, working with her was the ultimate pairing: my old-school ideas with her massive creativity.

I traveled home to Vermont every few weeks, but it wasn't enough. I was inattentive, so thrilled about my work that things began to take a slide (again). I contributed a lot to this, and I'm so sorry. My second marriage was coming to an end.

In Salt Lake, we collected résumés, videos, and tapes of hundreds of people who wanted to work at the 2002 Olympic Winter Games. We would be hiring for a number of positions, such as host-venue announcers, color commentators, French translators, and field talents who would work in-stadium, interacting with the spectators. We would also arrange and produce content for the video boards, organize precompetition music or talent, and conduct the flower ceremonies on-site. There was a lot to do, and not too much time to do

I Almost Made it

it. We hired music directors, DJs, and all manner of techs, and each venue had a producer who was responsible for pulling it all together.

I traveled to Montreal to hold an open casting call for French translators, which was fascinating, and we hired a number of them. Then traveled to New York to meet with the NHL about hiring some of their PA announcers from around the league.

We even hired the talented organist from Madison Square Garden, the kind Ray Costoldi, to play the organ at hockey games.

I lived in Park City and commuted daily to Salt Lake. It was a city that I came to love. Orderly, plenty of big-city amenities, but with a kind of small-town charm. And the people there were friendly and undyingly kind. After helping hire the announcers for the PA and making those recommendations to Christy, I settled in to announce cross-country skiing and ski jumping. I had learned enough at this point to be reasonably confident in my knowledge, abilities, and storytelling.

Then, again, out of the blue, came another call that was life altering. It was the famed, Emmy Award-winning producer from LA, Don Mischer. He asked if I would be willing to audition as the English-language stadium voice for the Olympic Opening and Closing ceremonies.

Peter Graves

Once again I said yes. And days later, I went over to KSL TV in Salt Lake to audition.

I read some copy, and later that day I was hired. Just like that. In many ways, this was the biggest and most profound announcing I would ever do.

We rehearsed in the days leading up to the Games until midnight. It was all perfectly choreographed by Don. I just had to read the script. Still, there were no margins for error, and I never enjoyed working in those all-or-nothing environments. I resigned myself to go slowly, not to overmodulate, and simply to read one sentence of my script at a time.

Most of the Olympic rehearsals were done late at night at Rice Eccles stadium on the campus of the University of Utah, starting at about 11 p.m. and extending until about 1 a.m. I wasn't fearful of those, as I was simply reading to an empty stadium, but just doing it helped ratchet down my anxiety. We had daily script updates dropped off to my SLOOC office, and I had to sign a confidentiality clause saying I would not disclose anything about what I had seen or heard.

While I knew I had to go through with this— and wanted to—I still felt tremendously vulnerable. That week, I talked to my therapist every day. It's amazing the dread I could conjure when I knew that three billion people across the universe would be watching the ceremonies—and my work—live. The only thing that stood in my way was a red cough button . . . yikes. This was an extraordinary position to put someone who suffered from a good degree of anxiety.

I had to look the fear of making a mistake squarely in its face, and I did. I was proud of it all, and especially that my parents (by that point living in a retirement community) could see the show live on TV. I was so very close to my parents, and I think I took this on as much to please and honor them. The enormity of this was pretty scary, but I knew I had to do it and look fear in the face. Truthfully, doing this huge, global event was a real response to all the bullies out there that had teased me. "I'll fucking show them," I thought.

In the end, it turned out perfectly, and I was deeply honored to be an inside part of the production. I did both the opening and closing for the Paralympic Games. I believed in a very idealistic view of the Olympic Games, and I still feel today that I was the right choice for that role. I was pretty scared, and yet it provided me with the simple yet profound life lesson: I tried and I didn't die.

That night, feeling great satisfaction, I skipped the cast party and enjoyed a root beer and burger at Hires in Salt Lake with Tom Kelly and his wife,

Carole. I just needed to feel normal again. Plus Hires had its classic fry sauce, a Utah tradition.

The rest of the Games, I announced on the PA for cross-country skiing and ski jumping. It felt wonderful to be doing a Games on home snows in the Watsatch.

I was teamed up in cross-country with the Norwegian master who was to become a cherished friend, Kjell Erik Kristiansen. His knowledge of the world's elite skiers was formidable, for he did many of the World Cups overseas. I sat in comfortably in the booth and become a strong second to him. I trusted him and learned from him. It was another great experience, as I let go of my ego and went with the flow.

HARVARD SKIING

12

When I returned to Putney following the 2002 Olympic Winter Games in Salt Lake City, I was without a job. So I started looking. I saw an ad in Ski Racing magazine for a Head Nordic coach position and applied on a lark—and I was hired.

After all those years, I became a Harvard man. I was proud to be there, and I had the chance to build the program from the ground up. For many reasons, being at Harvard was a real thrill and also a challenge. I encountered some extraordinary student athletes. Most of them just turned out to be on the team, and many had never even raced before. Most of them had never skied before. One of my skiers fell off the elevated start ramp in his first race. I knew I was in for a steep growth curve as I tried to build the program. It would take time.

I wore the Crimson H with pride, ordered new parkas, a new wax tent, and training apparel. We lifted weights three times a week, and everyone improved over time. It was a special moment in my life and I felt useful.

I wanted to build a team and a program, so my door was always open. To tell you the truth, I'm rather proud of it. Some of those kids had no business being on a Division I ski team, and yet here they were. And for a number of them, the introduction to the sport, its training patterns, and the carnival circuit was life altering in the most positive ways. I was proud of all of them. They were experimenting and, in many cases, it took great courage to go up against the big-gun skiers at UVM, Middlebury, and Dartmouth.

One thing was clear to me in retrospect: I had been out of real coaching since the mid-1980s, and while my skill set was fine for beginning racers, I probably lacked some of the more current, cutting-edge ability to coach top-flight skiers. That's probably right. Still, many and most didn't require that level of coaching. My last year there, some of the kids got together and, through various channels

I Almost Made It

and reviews, let me and the athletic department there know it. I must say the reviews were stinging to me, but ultimately, I made the decision in 2008 to retire from coaching. My parents were in the slow process of dying in an assisted living home in Vermont, and I thought I neither needed the aggravation nor the time suck that went into the job. I was not without fault in leaving Harvard, and I still consider it a good move. I'm close with many of the skiers I coached, and take pride in their involvement in the sport. I'd like to think my mentorship and full-on approach to the sport helped motivate them to carry forth.

In February of 2008, while driving back from the Middlebury College Carnival in Vermont, I received a phone call from Tom Kelly that was to be life changing. Our long and dear friend, Paul Robbins, had been found dead that afternoon in his Vermont home. Paul and I were close, really close. We met in 1978 and became fast friends, and we shared many mutual interests: journalism, politics, music, skiing, and a love of Vermont. For a short time after I left ESPN, Paul took over as an analyst, and that led to him being hired by CBS to work at the Nagano and Albertville Winter Olympic Games for CBS Sports. I never felt betrayed by Paul, and we talked about the subject openly and often for

Peter Graves

a while. He knew me too well to know that being replaced wasn't without pain. I loved him too much to let that stand in the way of a beautiful friendship.

"PR" was whip smart, quick on his feet, and great with one-liners (far better than me, for I never felt I was either funny or quick), and he impressed the network brass. He also had the advantage of working with one of the most gifted announcers I have ever had the pleasure of meeting, Al Trautwig. The duo couldn't fail.

That led, for Paul, to Olympic gigs in Salt Lake City and Torino, for which he did admirably. He was the dean of American Nordic journalists, and the former sports announcer at Boston's WRKO radio, and former Boston bureau chief at UPI. He was widely respected. It's funny how things go; we had talked not long before his passing about death. Perhaps he felt it encroaching, but he said one day that if I survived him to please take his ashes to the next Olympics I went to and sprinkle them about the press room and the ski trails. With his son David, ("DC," to many), Tom Kelly, and a few others, we did just that and honored him in the way he wanted.

In fact, Paul's ashes have been widely traveled, for I have always carried some with me wherever I have journeyed, a courtesy of DC. But the bulk of his remains are in a Dunkin' Donuts box at his widow, Kathe's, home. At least what's left after ceremonial sprinklings at the finish line at Beaver Creek and other places important to him. It was PR that got the last laugh for his truly iconoclastic sense of humor. He would have loved it all. I think of him every day. And the classic reminder, "What would Paul Do?" continues to guide me.

Paul was one of a kind. And the sport was slightly less fun with his passing.

*The deepest craving of all human beings
is the desire to be appreciated.*

—William James

OLN, The Outdoor Life Network, was a fledgling start-up network based in Stamford, Connecticut, run by a former coordinating producer of mine at ESPN, Peter Englehart. I always liked Peter and appreciated his intellect, so when I heard OLN was buying up the FIS rights to skiing, I got in touch. This led to a phone call with a man I had heard about, who had won two Emmy Awards and praise at ABC Sports, Ric LaCivita. Ric had come from CBS Sports, where he garnered a reputation as a tough taskmaster and demanding producer. The Harvard-educated LaCivita was also a two-sport star athlete for the

Crimson, in soccer and baseball. Ric made me feel appreciated. Still does.

While some might have mistaken his demandingly high standards for real aggressiveness, I was truly captivated by his passion for athletes and sports and for his love of language and storytelling. I liked him immediately. We bonded quickly and have since become lifelong friends. I respect him immensely. As I mentioned, Ric prized good storytelling, which I was also quite good at, and he encouraged me to sharpen my chops in that area. I learned about tone and texture in my storytelling. I learned so much from him. What's more, I'm still to this day extremely grateful for his able guidance. "Educate, inspire, and inform" were his watchwords for good television.

In addition to being an "announcers' producer," LaCivita had a probing eye for young, unvarnished talent, and he gave career boosts to many youthful announcers and producers who were looking for their big break in the business of sports television. Among only a handful, "Las" preferred to pay it forward. My time in Stamford at OLN saw me host skiing programs of all kinds for the network and work with a bevy of right-out-of-college producers who are now stalwarts at the major networks.

I worked with the talented Greg Lewis, who

worked for NBC Sports, and the former Alpine skiing star Pam Fletcher, both of whom were fun, bright, and easy to work with. At that time I was also traveling the globe doing the PA announcing at UCI World Cup mountain biking, something I had done since the late 1980s as a freelance job. So OLN acquired the Mountain Bike World Cup rights, and I would do shows from Cape Town to Arai, Japan; from Austria to Australia. It was an amazing experience. The downside to it all was that the extraordinary amount of traveling I did took me away frequently from my then-wife and my kids, Katie and Willy, who were very young then. Despite my love for my work, I had a nagging sense of guilt when I was away. I had always wanted to be a good father.

All the while, I was engaged in a master class of television production.

We did set shots, studio programs, and work on location. I learned how to read a teleprompter, apply the right shade of makeup, and how to have a polished studio presence. It was great fun and I took to it quickly.

It was Ric that understood and went after the rights to the annual Tour de France, giving it real-time, all-day coverage. Just the kind of race fans wanted and deserved in the States. He brought in heavyweight announcers Phil Liggett and (the now-late) Paul Sherwin, and added the offbeat Bob "Bobke" Roll, a former Tour rider and mountain bike racer, for just the right touch of levity. Ric's genius was once again on display in how he crafted the shows, the TV rights, and the talent, and he deserved major credit for making it happen. Ric always made me feel good and confident, and I thrived under his direction. Most of all, I believed in him.

Just like so many other times, one day into my third year at OLN, I got a call from Ric letting me know he was resigning as executive producer and would be moving on. Once again, I could feel the air draining out of my sunny balloon. And after some management changes, OLN would now morph into Versus, and they were after big "gets" in the rights-fee department, notably in ice hockey.

After Ric departed, his replacement was John Carter, who immediately cut back my hours for OLN and had a different view of the network. While on the verge of having real TV sports exposure for my work and the growing confidence that I could play with the big boys, I was going to have to reinvent myself at another network, and there was not a huge number of choices.

ATHENS

14

If you've gotten this far, you should know that for more than a decade, I was referred to as the "Voice of Mountain Biking." Again it was time to travel the globe in that pursuit. Fresh off the heels of the very successful Winter Games in Salt Lake, I was hired to do all cycling in English on the loudspeaker for the Athens 2004 Olympic Summer Games. I spent almost all of the building-up period for those Games doing research. Athens was the ancestral home of the modern Olympic Games and first held the Olympic Games in 1896, and then again in 2004. For anyone who loves Olympic history, this was a special place to return to.

The 2004 Games featured 10,557 athletes, and

their motto was a clever: "Welcome Home." I arrived a week or so before the Games were to start. Since this was the second Games under the specter of 9/11, security was extremely tight. The price tag for security alone was a hefty $1.2 billion. NATO forces were summoned to play backup should there be a terrorist attack. They were decamped nearby on the island of Evia, close to the capital city.

As I arrived, there was a flurry of activity in and around all the venues, and the organizers were candid, saying not all the work would be completed by the Games' start time. There were open hostilities between the many factions working on the Games. I went to an old, slightly undone hotel near the city center. A tiny room, but it did offer CNN and blessed air-conditioning in the heat and humidity of summer. We took our breakfast there. It was simple, but clean. Outside, each night, were a group of sex workers, anxious to ply their trade. I, of course, paid them no mind.

The Games themselves also provided many much-needed upgrades to the airport, the roadways, and a new citywide tram. This was unlike other Games, where corporate money from sponsorships would help foot the huge bill. I recall much dirt and no grass surrounded the Velodrome for track cycling. Give the organizers

I Almost Made it

an A for ingenuity, for as I walked into the track, officials were spray-painting that brown dirt into green, and frankly it wasn't half bad. I was to be assigned to road cycling, held downtown, while the mountain biking was held at Mount Parnitha, and the time trial was in the lush suburb of Vouliagmeni. It was there that I had the honor of calling Tyler Hamilton's gold medal run. I was proud when they played our national anthem so far away from home. Tyler would ride professionally on the road for a number of teams, most notably for Lance Armstrong's US Postal Service team. Tyler rode in service to Lance. Tyler was the only US rider to win one of the biggies of the sport, the fabled Liège-Bastogne-Liège in Belgium. He was a brilliant and talented rider.

Other than the work itself, my greatest memory of the Games was having a lovely, intimate dinner with cycling broadcast legends Phil Ligget and Paul Sherwin. We dined in the Old Town, with breathtaking views of the stunning 5th-century BC landmarks, the Acropolis and the Parthenon, overhead. Never did the time go so fast, as both men regaled me with inside stories of cycling history, including the Tour de France. Our dinner became a master's class for me, and I listened eagerly and with rapt attention.

I liked the Greeks immediately. They are a fun-loving people and deeply patriotic. Finally, the curtain went down on these historic Games, and I was the better for having been invited.

ON TO WCSN, UNIVERSAL, AND NBC SPORTS

15

Some of you are successes and some are failures. And only God knows which are which.

—ALEXANDER WOOLLCOTT

Obituaries are something I have always enjoyed reading. I suppose it was my late father's favorite section of the New York Times, as it became mine. There we note tales of high achievement, those we consider winners in the game of life. Yet obits often conceal the true stories of a person's life. For they often fail to list the defeats in favor of the victories.

As the 21st century dawned, I was ready, and a bit worried as I turned 50, if I would still have the drive to make things happen.

While I had worked at ESPN and ABC, and done a number of Olympic Games for them, my route to NBC, the Peacock network, was circuitous.

My friend Tom Kelly, then a Vice President at the US Ski Team, told me about an upcoming enterprise that was largely web-based at first, called WCSN (World Championships Sports Network). This was around 2005. WCSN was to carry loads of FIS ski programming. And that was just the ticket for me. Rights fees for skiing would come to them cheap, and except for the Olympic Games, most of the skiing programming was never aired in this country. There would be a vast amount of cross-country, biathlon, ski jumping, and Alpine programming. At some point, ESPN dropped all their ski coverage that I had done, so as not to help NBC build a market share for their Olympic programming. ESPN focused on the X Games as a source of their winter sports program.

I was hired via Claude Ruibal, one of the brain trusts who helped found WCSN and a good guy. Along with his sidekick producer, David Qualls, we all hit it off and they seemed pleased to have me on board. While a few early shows were produced in New York, most of them were done at the dark and dank Andrita Studios in the Los Angeles suburb of Glendale. So I drove my rental car from LAX through the attendant gate, past the razor wire; parked my car, and went in. No one gets into the building by accident. Again, it made for a great deal of traveling from Boston's Logan to LAX. Still, I got all those United and Hilton points!

The studio was also the de facto home of the Playboy Channel, complete with a sound stage where soft porn would be taped. It was not uncommon to bump into Christy Canyon or Ginger Lynn in the lunch room. It was a very strange place. A very strange place. I recall going into the master control one time to see mind-numbing porn being sent out to the satellites. Wow, a different world. But I was here to do Nordic skiing; it was a far cry from saunas and maple syrup, and I had walked into another world. Later, the stage and cast for the soap opera All My Children moved from New York to the building, and I recall seeing Susan Lucci and others in the halls. I felt like I had left bucolic Vermont and landed on the moon.

Despite that, WCSN had their own studio and voice over booths, and with an eager group of young production folks, we went to work. Some of them have now made it big in their own right at various networks.

Many flights from Boston to LAX and Burbank later, I had done hundreds of shows. I felt we were moving forward the Nordic skiing ball on television in the US. Never was there so much material out there, up until then. While I got a few nasty emails from several Nordies (there were Peter Graves haters? I never knew!), most people loved the coverage. It was the beginning of on-line forums and—funny me—I thought people would be pleased to have XC skiing and jumping on the air. But some of the comments were both cruel and biting. I didn't say the name right, or my analysis was off base. At least Howard Cosell got only letters that his secretary could throw away before he read them. Until then, I didn't realize how cruel this whole scene could be. But still, it was intoxicating. For here I was again, on a plane, on a taxiway, off for Burbank or LAX.

Our producer was a young, cheerful man named Dean Walker, who gave direction and was a delight to be around. The atmosphere in the studio was light, and it brought out the best in me. In that orbit I wasn't fearful of a mistake. We could always do another take, as most shows weren't live. I knew I worked best in that environment, and I wasn't looking over my shoulder about who might replace me. They seemed happy; so was I.

Still, I could have fifty great emails about the shows I had done, and if I had one negative one, it would ruin my day. This is not the best of traits in the business.

It went on that way for several years. I could have been in fat city. I didn't like the travel, but I got plenty of support from my third wife, Cami, to go and do something I loved. I was growing in confidence. Further, I was making some good bank. Up until one day I heard a bit of news.

The NBCUniversal family was going to purchase WCSN and use the rights and assets to develop a 24-hour sports network, which first became Universal Sports and later became NBCSN. Yet as soon as NBC Sports became involved, the stakes were higher. There was more tension in the studio and, frankly, a more demeaning style towards announcers like me.

A sure sign that nothing stays the same, the network suits had always made me nervous. They all had their own agendas—as well they should—but just like at ESPN, I could envision a time when they would "move in a different direction."

The executive producer was a man I only knew by reputation. From then on, little I did was right. We were always changing, or prodding. A word here—a phrase there. To be completely fair, that is the role of a producer: to make you better. Even announcers need to be pushed. Also, to be fair, I was working a very niche sport and was not even in the same league as Phil Liggett or Bob Costas, meaning I was the low man on the food chain. But the message was clear: he was nobody to mess with. He was a truly talented man whom I respected, but navigating this journey without a road map was tough not only for me but also for the likes of many niche sports announcers coming in from the hinterlands with little broadcast experience. I saw announcers there come and go. Some were let go immediately after doing one show. I was very uncomfortable witnessing some of this. Feeling that one day it would be me.

Every once in a while, it's nice to hear that you nailed it, got it right. But I didn't hear it. I soldiered on despite the scolding and accepted the treatment that I figured went along with the job description. Some producers lamented the lack of falls in modern day ski jumping. "It's not exciting anymore," they'd say. I tried to explain that after the Calgary Games the IOC instituted an "Eddie the Eagle Rule" that ostensibly locked out jumpers with limited international experience. World Cup and Olympic jumpers were all so good that falls had become rare. It soon began to feel, once again, like the survival-of-the-fittest dogma in sports TV. I was a sensitive and kind announcer who did not enjoy calling athletes out on national television, and more than a few times the producer told me to be more opinionated and tougher on the athletes. I recall myself saying, "You know, I live with these people, and it's not worth it to me to be too critical." I strived to be a decent, fair, and kind journalist, and felt very altruistic about the Olympic movement. I wasn't about to start being critical and disrespectful of people and their hopes and dreams.

I grew up under the spell of the legendary ABC Sports announcer Jim McKay, whose real name was McManus. He was respectful to a fault, undyingly kind and lovely to everyone. I idolized him, and wanted to be just like him. Hey, if someone's going to pick a role model in this business, you could do worse than pick Jim. Sometimes I wonder how he would have fared in today's cutthroat, smash-mouth-delivery environment that has become TV sports. He was gentle, even understated at times, and as I said, how he guided us through the Munich 1972 Summer Olympics, was a ready testament to his humility, his sense of humanity, and his utter decency. All done with damp swim trunks under his pants, summoned by Roone from his hotel swimming pool to immediately assume the anchor's chair. McKay was then at his very best. His gentle commentary on that dreadful day was simply a work of art.

One other thing about Jim. My parents' New York City friends Helen and Maron Simon (Maron a former *New York Times* journalist), who summered in Bennington, Vermont, were good friends of Jim's. And when I told Jim of that connection while we were in Lake Placid, he responded so sweetly in the affirmative. Yes, they were lovely people.

The clock at work, I could tell, was already ticking, even though the milieu hadn't changed. I was more nervous with every trip I made to the West Coast. I longed for respect and humanity, but my values were too high-minded.

I spent a few more years there, and weathered the move out of Andrita to the tony Four Seasons Hotel in West Lake Village. Of course the rooms were lovely, and the food opulent, but it was always trippy to me to come to work in this rather grand lobby in shorts and a T-shirt. Steve Schlanger hosted most of my shows then, while I served as analyst. Steve was a naturally talented announcer and I never saw anyone do more research or homework for a show, which was admirable. We got along fine.

During one of my trips, my wife, Cami, came with me. I'd do my work and she would shop or work out. We went to Catalina Island, and we had a red Mustang convertible that we cruised the Hollywood

Hills in. It was fun. Two native Vermonters were holding their own in LA. I thought of the time, travel, and research I had invested in all of this. I thought of how my travel had taken me away from home far too often, and it hurt.

As we were pulling into to the studio one day to park, in came another car, driven by a friend, Chad Salemla. To say I was surprised to see him was an understatement. We respected each other too much to be anything but polite and respectful. I asked what he was doing here; however, I supposed I already knew. He told me he was trying out for NBC as a Nordic skiing commentator and doing a few shows for them as a kind of audition.

Make no mistake: Chad, a former US biathlete, had every reason to be there, and the credentials to boot. Still, my heart sunk, for I knew that the clock was likely ticking faster at NBC, and my long-hoped-for dream, another shot at the upcoming Olympics in Vancouver in 2010, was likely to be dashed again . . . "Hey, we're going in a different direction."

Chad proved a fine choice to replace me. He was more current, more hip, and had a trained eye for the sport. Later, at the 2018 Olympic Games in Korea, he would nail cross-country skiing's most well-known race call during the gold-medal-winning event, featuring a breakthrough performance by America's Kikkan Randall and Jessie Diggins. He, along with Steve Schlanger, laid down XC's most famous track: "Here comes Diggins, here comes Diggins … " It was simply perfect.

Somewhat crushed by the circumstances, I recalled how I'd heard this before. I was so hoping to be on air in Vancouver. But I still scored a gig to PA the cross-country and jumping events as a co-announcer, which I still found enormously satisfying.

Yet, this was to be my last work with the Peacock Network until February of 2023, when I hosted World Cup ski jumping from Lake Placid. There are few exits in this business that are gracefully managed. Many announcers are fired or forced to retire. Some are asked to leave the building after being notified that their services are no longer needed.

Television is, at best, a fickle beast; and at its worst, it is terrifying, offering no stability. Yet it can be a wonderful storytelling tool when used well, and a strong narcotic for insecure people who are looking for fame, recognition, and praise. Make no mistake: those hiring talent are among the most sucked-up-to people anywhere, as they hold the keys to the announcing kingdom and the power to drop you in a New York minute. There are few happy endings.

When they decide to put you out to pasture, it can be a very subtle thing. When they need you, they call often; they want you right away. Conversely, when you are no longer needed, they stop calling. Or they stop answering your emails. "Yes, we're thinking about that," they will say, knowing full well you are done. "Yes, we may use you in Vancouver, maybe."

The doors were shutting. After all, I saw the way Frank Gifford, also one of the good guys in TV sports who gave his life to the ABC enterprise, had been dumped so cruelly. Fired by some production assistant he didn't know. None of the big executives at ABC/ESPN dared tell him. After his brilliant career, it showed a complete disregard to him. To say the least, they were not forthcoming. He deserved better.

Let's face it: if they could do it to Gifford, they could easily do it to Graves. Giff and I had become friends at the Lake Placid Games, and then reconnected later when I worked part time for the wonderful Special Olympics movement as their director of Nordic skiing. It was hard not to like Frank, and his kindness to the Special Olympic movement was legendary. I also admired Frank immensely for his grace under the withering criticism of a pair of cruel Howard Cosell books that took to task Giff's skill and talent as a broadcaster. He kept his mouth shut, and soldiered on and was terribly kind to Cosell during Howard's final illness—something that Cosell probably didn't deserve. But that was Frank, a genuine golden-boy-turned-broadcaster, who was reliably talented and kind.

So I hosted the PA team at Vancouver in 2010 for both cross-country and ski jumping, in what were truly great Games. Well organized and fun. What's more, since the venue for both of those sports was in Whistler, the living was good and easy.

OFF TO HOLMENKOLLEN: A DREAM COME TRUE

16

With the Vancouver Games in my rearview mirror, I was to have one of my professional life's truly meaningful experiences in February of 2011. I was asked by my friend to travel to Oslo to help announce the fabled Holmenkollen, which doubled as the 2011 FIS Nordic World Ski Championships. I was so thrilled. I doubt there has ever been an American who announced on the PA there. To have my voice over the loudspeaker at this venue would truly make me feel like, after all these many years, I had arrived. Every Nordic competitor knows and appreciates the mystique and allure of this venue, and every Nordic skier considers it the holy grail of the sport. It was truly a dream. My friend, the now-late Mike Gallagher, told me when I arrived at Holmenkollen to kiss the snow, and I did just that. The entire two weeks felt like I was in a Nordic wonderland.

The Holmenkollen festival started in 1892 and has been going on ever since. Many of my age might well have had adorned their walls with pictures of Mickey Mantle or Ted Williams; mine was plastered with the Holmenkollen posters and their Norwegian greats. During each annual March festival, the event truly becomes the Super Bowl of Nordic skiing. Holmenkollen hosted the 1952 Olympic Winter Games, and the 1930, 1966, 1982, and 2011 FIS Nordic World Ski Championships. The winners there become legends of the sport. It is a source of national pride when a Norwegian wins there, and the natural soundtrack becomes complete with the ringing of cowbells and thousands of spectators waving Norwegian flags. It's a national party, for a nation with an inherent love of Nordic skiing.

Their 1952 Olympic Games attracted the largest crowds of any Olympic Games to date. Even the lifting of the torch was the stuff of legend. The lighting of the torch came from the fireplace hearth of the Norwegian great, Sondre Norheim. The Games were memorable for many reasons, but particu-

I Almost Made It

larly memorable to me were the performances of Vermont great Andrea Mead Lawrence, who won the slalom and giant slalom even though she was but nineteen years old.

I recall vividly Kjell Erik's advice: "You won't need to talk about waxing, training, or technique, the Norwegians already know that stuff . . . just make it fun and energetic." And I did just that. Now, really growing confident in my work, working in Oslo was a dream come true. To be asked to be one of the public-address announcers was a huge honor and one I'll never forget. I was over the moon.

KOREA: THE 13TH GAMES

17

*I am no longer concerned with good and evil.
What concerns me is whether my offering
will be acceptable.*

—Robert Frost (in his sixties)

Now into my sixties, I had grown much more contemplative about sport and the Olympic Games. Not that I still didn't enjoy the rush of working the Games, but now my folks had gone, and it was harder and harder to get around. Having been married for the third time in 2010, I still looked upon Cami to provide me strength and emotional support. By then, however, even she was questioning if going to another Games was worth the effort. For it's true that I would return home after the enormous effort of working at an Olympic Games bone weary and emotionally wiped out.

But I was fearful of retirement, and I often expressed to Cami that I'd rather die doing the

Olympics or on a compelling assignment than pass peacefully at home. Pass with my boots still on, given as these years of announcing still felt like I was chasing a dream. So again, in 2018, it was time for me to travel to Korea for the Olympics, though it was immediately after announcing the Birkie in Hayward, WI. I was already tired.

Korea was a very hard Games for me. Not that I didn't enjoy my work or have fun, but the physical toll it took on my body and mind was hard. The work was hard and exhausting, the food wasn't great, our lodging was far out of town, and our assigned drivers would only take us to the venues. We were stuck twenty kilometers away with no place to really eat or any way to get out after work and enjoy the Games. There was a gas station over a kilometer away I often walked to that served food. I reminded myself often that this was not NBC. My NBC friends asked me often, "How's the buffet at your place?" I reveled in telling them neither was there a buffet nor a front-desk concierge, or anything. We were out in the boonies for sure. And our place was more like a hostel. At the gas station I feasted upon such delights as hot dogs and cheese. There is a stark difference between being a network-TV announcer and a public-address one.

I Almost Made it

Ah, the glamour of it all! Kimchi and rice three times a day, putting my stomach and Yankee-white bowels in a tailspin. In Korea, at the Games, it was breakfast like that for a thousand people, all with the same serving ladle.

I was assigned to announce on the public-address system for the Alpine skiing events. There was little natural snow, mostly man made; and alongside the trails, the earth was brown and scattered with leaves. I had a good team to work with and the races went well. I worked closely with our producer, Marco, who was doing his first skiing event ever. Fortunately, he was a quick study, but still leaned into me for storylines and content. I was happy he was so truly interested.

I pulled my crumbling back out badly and was in real pain, and my arthritic legs were creaky and burning. I didn't sleep much. I was a mess, but I put up a good and strong front, like I always tried to do. No one knew how much I was hurting.

I was moved to tears the night Jessie Diggins and Kikkan Randall took the gold medal in the team sprint event. I watched it on Korean TV and it marked a huge milestone in the growth of the Nordic sport in North America. I was so proud of them. My thoughts drifted back to all those that weren't alive to see that night where we were on top of the world. It all marked an unforgettable moment in time.

Immediately after flying home, I went to the hospital for an epidural of soothing back-pain medication so I could keep working. And working then meant a turnaround after five days to Åre, Sweden, to do the PA for the Alpine World Cup Finals in Alpine skiing. The jet lag threw me for another loop. I was sleeping only three to four hours per night. Again, my work didn't suffer, but behind the scenes I was hurting. My mood grew poor. I was depressed and anxious. And, of course, I had no one to lean on. Announcing can be glamorous, but you still have to come back to a lonely hotel room, alone. By the time I returned home, I was completely drained, physically and emotionally. I didn't know what time zone I was in, and I went several weeks sleeping fitfully. It didn't help my mental state or my attitude. I couldn't help but wonder if all this was worth it—was I still chasing the brass ring and never grasping it? Fatigue always brought out some painful truths to me of what was really important in work and life.

I came back home for another five days and went to Craftsbury for the Super Tour. It was great to see the recently returned US Olympic Team fresh from their amazing season-long performances and the gold medal. I took odd comfort in knowing they must have been as tired and drained as I was, but I was amazed by how well they were all holding up, at least when they were performing.

I felt the black dog of depression really overtaking me. "What went wrong, what was the matter?" I questioned. I had never felt this drained or down. I went to the doctor and got some medication that helped me sleep a bit better. But my mood didn't lift.

I always loved my work, but now I was going through the motions. I wondered if anybody would notice. I was scared.

In the following weeks, I had foot surgery to remove a neuroma. I had a big cancerous growth taken off my back, which always scared me, that later migrated to my left armpit and stage-three metastatic cancer. It was perhaps my first brush with my own mortality. Yet, and thankfully, the surgery was a success and they seemed to get it all. For my delaying the radiation until after the Olympic Games, my oncologist called me a fool, and he might well have been correct. But the allure of the Games once again blinded me. The work meant the world to me. I had five weeks of radiation, and some of what I witnessed in the cancer clinic at Dartmouth was deeply moving. Sick, very sick children, surely dying, made me think less about myself. One little girl in particular was in bad shape and I struck up a friendship with her during our treatments. She was probably six and already wheelchair bound. We talked about the Olympics and traveling to far-flung places that I knew she would never see. I gave her a teddy bear from Korea and a ski hat, which she immediately embraced. I marveled at her immediate joy, and her courage. Then one day she was no longer there; she had died.

My knees hurt. I was getting a cataract in my right eye that made my vision blurry. I felt like I was falling apart. My frustrations about myself were horrible. This aging game was getting hard to take. I took some of it out on Cami, constantly pushing her to understand what I was feeling. It wasn't always very nice and I regret hurting her. I am still trying to learn that just because she was available, it didn't make it right or fair to unload on her. To me, it appeared that she had to take it; she was the only one I could be truly honest with. My actions often pushed her away, for which I'm sorry. After all these years, I'm still trying to learn ways to better regulate my pain, anger, and frustrations. This journey is not only lined with success, but suffering too. Every new Olympics, with its challenges, took me out of my comfort zone. And the clock was ticking.

I wanted someone to take pity on my state, understand completely, and make the pain go away. I guess what I really wanted was my mother, to hold me and say everything would be all right. Still, it was my father who had given me the gift of reading and poetry. He long ago had introduced me to the poems of Emily Dickinson, whose poem "Crumbling is not an instant's Act" seems particularly apt at this stage in my life. And so I enter the third act in this Grecian stage of my life. And yet, it is never too late, and one never knows what's around the bend.

THAT'S ALL FOLKS

18

Now into my seventies, I have grown much more contemplative about the meaning of sport and the Olympic Games. Looking back, I realize I often defined myself by life's circumstances. A freelancer most of my life, when I snagged a great job, things were terrific; when I was out of work, or lost a gig to someone else, I was blue. I often entertained thoughts that if I did a good show, I could contribute to making the world a better place through teamwork, sportsmanship, and global brotherhood. It all came down to what you did in that one moment in time where you captured the right word, or phrased something just right. Not all of us in this business have the opportunity to have such a moment to work with. Think of the talented Al Michaels with his poetic line, "Do you believe in miracles? Yes!" or Howard's, "Down goes Frazier, Down goes Frazier!" Or Chad's capturing of the moment of gold-medal joy in the call of "Here comes Diggins! Here comes Diggins!" in the 2018 Winter Games. They all captured a moment and made broadcast history that will live on forever.

I realize now that, for the most part, I shall never have the kind of adventures I've written about ever again. Though I continue to be mobile, I'm less likely to travel great distances by air, fight mind-numbing time zones and the battle to stay near the top. My work companions now are computers, and my good microphone I keep in my office for Zoom and Zencastr voice-overs. Often, from my living room, I call World Cup ski racing, which I adore.

But really, friends, for the most part it's been a pleasure and an honor. I've now worked at thirteen Olympic Games. Back in my youth, I never would have dreamed of that. I'm still working and loving it. I'll try and keep doing it until it ends—I love it that much.

Nonetheless, I have never felt like a particularly great success. In fact, it now surprises me that I have an extraordinary ability to underachieve. It was always my aggressiveness and work-hard ethic that made the difference. That and bran cereal.

I think if there was a skill I had, it was storytelling. I am ever mindful of what my producer-friend at OLN TV, Ric LaCivita said: "It's about sitting around the campfire." He's right, but the way much of television sports is going now, it's a dying art. There is virtually no forum for it any longer, except perhaps at the Olympic Games. But the way of Wide World of Sports no longer exists.

I have tried not to hold grudges, and I hope that I've been a good father, husband, and friend. Simple human values, to me, mean the most, and I'm now, more sure than ever, that life is simply a linked series of personal choices. And for me, my work helped define me. It gave me a sense of identity and even joy. I'm not certain that everyone in my life understood my dedication to my work, but it gave me something that nothing else provided. Being honored by the US Ski and Snowboard Hall of Fame was a great honor and proof that my work counted for something. Still, I was never motivated by prizes, awards, or inductions. I just wanted to do good work.

I wish I had more success as a husband, and it sears me to the bone. Never did I dream I'd be married three times, and I am ashamed by it. I did have the joy of being with three wonderful, kind, accomplished woman, all of whom helped me reach for the stars. Sadly, being somewhat insecure, I expected them to prop me up, until in every case it took its toll, and the near-constant traveling didn't help. I hope, somehow, they will find it in their hearts to forgive me, but that might be too much to ask. I'll simply say, "I'm in your debt."

The future of television sports as we know it is in great turmoil, and I could guess where we will end up. Now I've engaged in broadcasting live from my home, covering skiing on my computer, just me solo for two or three hours—live—basically without a producer, and no boots on the ground. It helps that I've been to many of these venues before, but it is a challenge—and all to a very knowledgeable audience for ski and snowboarding live. The man who has been hiring me is a charming fellow, Tom Read, from New York. This pay-per-view concept is where we are likely headed. We don't control the cameras, so what the world-feed gives us is what we have to work with. It's still fun, but as my career wanes, I don't know how much longer I'll be at this. At seventy-one, the years have taken their toll. I have always thought I'd know when the time was right to make my leave. I don't want to overstay my welcome, and be like the washed-up comedic acts

I Almost Made it

playing Vegas or the Catskills. Still, I've never lost interest in telling stories and covering events.

For me, the business of sports television is also better now than those halcyon days. There is more respect from producers, less screaming, and a calmer attitude which we have hard won. While the producers are younger, the good ones are still around and know how to bring out the best in their talent. I enjoy working with these young people, especially among the current crop. The talented Spence Viola from Echo Entertainment really has a way of storytelling and getting the best from his announcers. My live-show producer on jumping, former Olympian Kris Severson, is as good as it gets in the ski-jumping booth. Kent Gordis, a highly educated Yalie, still makes me laugh and does a great job. I prize his friendship still. He loves the Olympic movement.

It seems I have dedicated a great deal of life to the Olympics, from aspiring athlete to coach, and NGB administrator to TV and PA announcer. I am honored, along with thousands of others, to have played a small part in the overall milieu of the Games. Despite the attendant problems of doping and a few others, the Games still bring us together on a (hopefully) common playing field. And given the state of the world currently, I believe the Games are needed now more than ever. They unite us. They bring us together. And while insiders may almost constantly bicker over many nuanced issues, they provide us with a common bond. Sports are no more and no less than music, the arts, the advances in medicine and science. They are my world, and without this every-four-year gathering, we would all be the lesser for it. In a sense, the Olympic Games are like a public trust. They belong to all of us.

Issues of using the Games in propaganda, as Hitler did in the Summer and Winter Games of 1936, was an abysmal use of power to showcase a fascist regime. Nonetheless, we survived it, and the Games moved forward. The murder of Israeli athletes in Munich was a tragic and terrible low point in Games history; still, the Games continued. The tragedy of that still moves me to this day, and likely always will. The Olympic Games must survive as a global movement, and they need to be constantly nurtured.

There have been breakthrough performances associated with the Olympics since it started, and all of them remarkable: a country's first medal, showing us the meaning of courage. It reminds me of the courage and bravery of Jackie Robinson breaking the color line in Major League Baseball, leaving a sports legacy that will live on in all our

I Almost Made it

hearts. Or Ali lighting the Olympic flame in Atlanta in 1996, despite a debilitating disease. They all add up to the sum total of what sports can give us. It's a great benefit.

The future, I just don't know. There still might be something, but nowadays, I don't hold my breath. The phone doesn't ring as often as it used to. But now I'm just trying to live and be a good person. Over the years, I kept a diary of sorts of my work and travels, jotting on planes the many different restaurants where I ate, almost always alone and the like. Looking back, I did have a pretty good run, and I'm proud of that. Recently in a book I was reading, I found a quote from the noted oceanographer and filmmaker Jaques Cousteau that, to me, sums up it up perfectly: "When one man, for whatever reason has the opportunity to lead an extraordinary life, he has no right to keep it to himself." I liked that very much.

Still, I have only a few regrets, and the high points outweigh the low by a great deal. I've seen the world, made great friends, and experienced some truly extraordinary moments. Still I can't help but feel like . . .

I almost made it.

AFTERWORD

Now that I have book one under my belt and realize how much work and editing goes into a project like this, I continue to have a flood of memories of what to put in and what to leave out.

One thought came to me today for which I am proud of, and I wanted to share. It's not intended in anyway to be political, but it is a very human story. At the 2002 Olympic Winter Games, as you know, Kjell-Erik Kristiansen and I were doing the live PA call. Sometimes you wonder if our commentary after a while gets tuned out and reduced to what we call "white noise"

It was the men's 20km pursuit race at Soldier Hollow and the field was complete with the best skiers on the planet. We called the winners nobly, but there was one skier who never landed on the podium, and perhaps went unnoticed. The last couple of skiers at the back came in after a long trudge on tough trails. One of those was the skier from the Islamic Republic of Iran, Mostafa Mirhashemi. His performance was expectedly unnoteworthy, but he finished in 79th position. Shortly before the games President Bush declared Iran as an "axis of evil," for which he may have been quite right. I figured no one would cheer Mostafa in, and I was pretty much right.

Quickly I was overcome in the spirit of goodwill and sportsmanship, and I put forth some nice words of encouragement, including, "let's welcome our friend in sport to the finish," and "let's give him a big cheer."

A chorus of cheers followed. It's not often, especially during those turbulent times, that Americans would cheer for an Iranian skier, but surprisingly they did. I'm glad I did that. This was about sport not politics, and I smiled to think that Mostafa might bring some positive words back to his homeland. I think you often build goodwill one person at a time, and hopefully he went home thinking that the Yanks gave him a warm welcome. For me it was a great send off and a lovely memory.

ACKNOWLEDGMENTS

I am grateful to all the people who made this journey with me. Notably, Ric Lacivita, who made my work better. Gary Larson, John Morton, and John Caldwell. I am also thankful for my life- long friendship with Scott Broomhall, who keeps the sport real for me, and grateful there are people like John Estle who is so competent and loves cross country so much. He has made a huge impact on the sport. I am also grateful for the huge number of volunteers who help run races across the country whose selfless efforts have helped the sport grow in the United States. Without them we couldn't have the high quality races we have. They all share in the matrix of our current success of the U.S. Ski Team. Bravo. All my coaches. Scott Keenan, for his loyalty at Grandma's Marathon. My lifelong friends, Robin

Outwater and Tom Kelly. And my friends at ABC Sports and ESPN.

I also want to thank John Morton, Dennis Donahue, and JD for the wonderful discussions and hot saunas. I also want to thank superb announcer and friend Chad Salmela for his input and Kent Gordis, the erudite Yalie, who had been a long-time producer of mine, not only for his skill but also his ability to crack me up with good humor when I needed it most. That includes the late ski journalist Paul Robbins. Thanks to the late Tom Corbin of Anchorage, who had been a long-time friend and advisor since I met him on the Long Trail Hike in Vermont years ago. He turned so many people onto the sport. The late duo of Mike Gallagher and Mike Elliott taught me lessons on toughness, camaraderie, and the importance of team even in an individual sport, and my lifelong friends Robin and Meg Outwater, Eric Evans (himself an Olympian) for our deep conversations regarding the Olympic movement and the state of televised sports, Chris and Mary for their warm friendship and the legendary coach Sven Wiik, who coached several of my coaches Bucky and Dolph. The late Al Merrill at Dartmouth. And thanks to Rumford friends like Dan Warner, Rick Hale and Monkey and the brilliant athlete and coach, the late Chummy Broomhall, and my friends at ABC Sports and

ESPN for their intellectual brilliance and skill, and so many more.

And to all my friends, who inspired me—you know who you are. Thanks so very much.

I am grateful to my editor, Rose Alexandre-Leach, for taking my jottings and making them better. Also, thanks to Dede Cummings, publisher at Green Writers Press, and Dana Sprague for introducing us.

I am truly grateful for the love I have shared with Kate and Mark, my grandson James Bowen, my son Willy and his wife Jada Lindbloom—the loves of my life—and my late parents, Van and Ella Graves, for their wisdom.

ABOUT THE AUTHOR

For over fifty years, Peter Graves, a native of Bennington, Vermont, has been a storyteller, writer, television sports host, and public address announcer, all put into play by his passion for cross country skiing at high school and college.

Graves has been an assistant coach for the US Ski Team and was the Head Nordic Coach at Harvard University, and the Nordic Sports Director for

Special Olympics International. He also worked to get the Giants Ridge Ski Area in northern Minnesota off the ground and played a major role in their historic World Cup.

His first winter Olympic Games he worked for ABC Sports at the 1980 games in Lake Placid, New York, covering Nordic Skiing. At the time of publication, Graves has announced at 13 Olympic Games, both Summer and Winter.

His work has appeared on ABC Sports, NBC/ Universal Sports, ESPN, OLN, CTV and CBC in Canada, and countless podcasts in this modern era.

Graves has two grown children: Kate, a former Nordic racer at Putney School and now an organic farmer, and former US Ski Team member in Nordic Combined, Willy.

He is a honored member of the US Ski and Snowboard Hall of Fame and The Vermont Ski Hall of Fame.

He resides in the Upper Valley of Vermont.